THE LANDLORD CHRONICLES

Investing in Low and Middle Income Rentals

Written by

Barbara Barnes Getty

authorHOUSE®

AuthorHouse™
1663 Liberty Drive
Bloomington, IN 47403
www.authorhouse.com
Phone: 1-800-839-8640

First published by AuthorHouse 6/30/2010

ISBN: 978-1-4520-4237-4 (sc)
ISBN: 978-1-4520-4238-1 (hc)
ISBN: 978-1-4520-4239-8 (e)

Library of Congress Control Number: 2010909230

Printed in the United States of America
Bloomington, Indiana

This book is printed on acid-free paper.

FORWARD

Barb Getty knows her stuff. It was a real treat for me to read her book on rentals. The thing that struck me the most is that, starting from almost nothing, she has been able to accumulate an impressive portfolio of properties in a relatively short period of time.

One of the more interesting parts of Barb's experience is her approach through the "low end" of the market. This has special appeal because that part of the market is especially accessible to first time investors with limited capital and a desire to provide for their own future; not a bad thought, considering the likely future of Social Security and Medicare.

Her approach, you will note, is long on elbow grease and short on hired help. This is the secret to her great returns on equity. Like most successful people, Barb is a self made woman. The only limitation on her potential is the time she can spend on her work. When she becomes maxed out, I expect she will parlay her single family units into multiple family complexes and continue to grow.

Her story should serve as an inspiration to those of you that want a secure future and are willing to work for it. I hope you enjoy the book and profit from it.

Stuart Leland Rider
Scottsdale, Arizona
3/8/2010

Stuart Leland Rider is a commercial real estate developer and general contractor. He has written seven books on real estate investing, including *The Complete Idiot's Guide to Real Estate Investing* and *The*

Complete Idiot's Guide to Investing In Fixer-Uppers. He recently co-authored with Getty on a book entitled *After the Bubble: Profit from Your Home and Affordable Rentals.*

TABLE OF CONTENTS

Sweat trickled down my back and soaked my waistband. I'd signed all the papers, handed over the money, and the seller's realtor was pushing the duplex keys across the table toward me. Although I'd done my "homework," (read various books about real estate investing and landlording, talked with other investors, etc.) a large part of me wanted to back out and go home. I was just plain scared.

The events that precipitated my sitting at this closing table were tragic and unexpected. Real estate investing was never, ever part of the plan. Though college educated, I'd stayed home to raise my three kids, ages 17, 16 and 14, and did free-lance artwork for a little extra cash. Our family's existence was shattered when, one beautiful day in August 1992, our 17-year-old son Todd was killed in an automobile accident. Eight months later, my 21-year marriage ended. My girls (Anne and Allison) were struggling to cope with the loss of a big brother they adored and reeling from the blow of their parents' divorce. In addition to dealing with my own unbearable grief, I was faced with the overwhelming challenge of finding an affordable home in which my girls and I could live. For the sake of Anne and Allison, I needed to keep them in their home school, and there were very few homes in my price range.

What I ended up with was a 1970's ranch-style beauty 1/3 the size of our former home, with dark, dingy paneling, funky green shag carpet, and yellow-gold appliances. Upon seeing the inside shortly after I bought it, Anne was aghast.

"Oh my God! You mean I actually have to *live* here?" (Aah, teenagers…)

I responded, "It just needs a little work, that's all. Don't worry, it'll be fine."

I was a bit nauseous at the thought of trying to make this work out. All the bravado in the world couldn't calm my fears. Actually, being on my own with two teenage daughters was enough challenge in itself.

Fortunately, our home needed mostly cosmetics, such as paint, new flooring and some creativity. It required $10,000 plus "sweat equity," but when completed, the former "dump" looked, in Anne's words, "Totally awesome!" and I live there still.

As I mentioned above, real estate investing was never part of the plan. Following my divorce, I was backed into a financial corner. My artist income was meager, and my teaching license had lapsed years ago. Getting re-certified would require taking classes over a period of time. Because my own home turned out well, friends suggested I buy run-down homes and fix them up to sell, as a source of income for myself. However, as my accountant pointed out, buying and fixing up to resell is *not* a guaranteed deal. If the home doesn't sell for awhile, there's no income. She suggested I buy something, fix it up and rent it out, which would provide us with a small but steady source of income.

Although I was struggling in many areas of my life (grieving Todd's death, worried about my girls' emotional well being, facing the dissolution of my marriage, moving from our family home, fearful about our financial future), I had to do *something*. So, we fast forward to that closing table…

Ignoring my damp shirt, I said my good-byes, grabbed the keys to my new duplex, and headed out the door.

CHAPTER ONE
WHAT'S YOUR NICHE?

SO, HAVE YOU ALREADY purchased that first rental, or are you merely toying with the idea? Either way, you've picked up the right book. I wish I'd had a hands-on guide to help me stumble through it all, several years ago. At age 46, one might think middle-aged wisdom would see me through. Unfortunately, *no*. Even though I read everything I could get my hands on, I still managed to make just about every mistake in the book. The goal of this book is to save you from repeating those same mistakes.

Since embarking on this journey, I've been approached by a variety of individuals who want information and advice about starting up their own real estate investing career. They're people who:

- Are newly divorced or widowed
- Are in their 20s and 30s and want to supplement their income
- Are in their 40s and 50s , looking to escape the 9-to-5 grind associated with their jobs
- Are unemployed due to downsizing at their companies
- Have faced discrimination in the corporate world and decided to control their own destiny by striking out on their own
- Are in high income tax brackets and want to take advantage of the incredible tax breaks available to real estate investors
- Have taken early (or even late) retirement, in good health, and are "re-inventing" themselves as they take a new direction in the business world

1

Real estate investing is an attractive alternative for a wide variety of individuals. Unlike many other business ventures, it's possible to get started with very little money. The beauty is that, as you're earning income from the rental, the value of the home is (hopefully) increasing each year. A wise purchase will provide you with income quickly, but is also a growth investment over the long haul.

Over the past few years, we've seen a plateau in home prices, and in places where the market was soaring, there's been a significant drop in price. Thousands of foreclosures are appearing in the real estate market throughout the country. Savvy investors are taking advantage of the situation. With foreclosures on the rise and credit becoming more elusive for people with less than stellar credit scores, a greater number of Americans will be forced into rental homes instead of becoming buyers; the demand for rentals will increase. The current climate represents a tremendous opportunity for the smart investor who is interested in getting into rental properties.

Do you enjoy people? Are you willing to listen and learn from others? Are you good about record keeping? Does the idea of running your own show excite you? If you're willing to participate in the rehab process and manage your properties on your own, this book will provide you with a simple, solid plan that will ensure personal and financial freedom for you. Sound crazy? It's not. Most people I know spend their lives working the daily grind, taking very few vacations or days off, hoping their pensions or social security will be there for them when they retire. Doesn't sound very uplifting, does it?

My close friend Darren has several single-family homes in this area. He's built his portfolio over several years and although he's only in his mid-thirties, he has a lot of free time on his hands. He's busy through the first week and a half of the month when rents are due, but aside from move-outs and occasional repair issues, he's on the proverbial Easy Street. With his spare time, he's vacationing with his family and starting up another business. Not because he needs the money to survive, but because his entrepreneurial spirit is leading him there. With this type of investing, it's very possible to earn full-time income and put in part-time hours. It's a beautiful thing.

When I began purchasing rental property, I didn't have much money to invest in the venture, so I looked at low-priced homes. I also researched the rental market itself. According to the 2004 U.S. Census, 40.3% of American households earn less than $35,000 per year. Of that 40.3%, more than a quarter earn $25,000 or less. A large portion of people in these income brackets will be renters for life – creating a stable long-term market, offering tons of opportunity for someone like me, or you. Armed with this information, I began my search for a low-priced home in need of a little TLC.

Please note: Inexpensive rentals are not synonymous with slums! There are thousands of affordable rental properties being rented by decent, hardworking Americans whose income places them in low and middle-income brackets. The focus of this book will be on those types of rental properties.

SINGLE-FAMILY: GET YOUR FEET WET

You may want to consider buying a single-family rental property if you already have a full-time job or other obligations that take a fair amount of your time. Also, if risk-taking isn't something you embrace, the single-family option will feel less like jumping off a bridge than a duplex.

It's less labor-intensive to buy the single family home, for the following reasons:

- It's easier to manage one tenant, rather than two or three, under one roof
- The tenant will pay their own utilities, may be on a one-year lease, and will pay the rent by the month, rather than weekly or bi-weekly
- In most cases, a single-family home takes less time (and money) to rehabilitate

Buying a single-family rental will give you a taste of what it's like to be a landlord, and if you decide you've made the worst mistake of your life, selling that home may be easier than trying to get rid of a multi-family dwelling.

However, there's a down side to the single-family, middle-income home. If mortgage interest rates take a dive, your tenants may explore the possibility of buying their own home, and you'll be looking for new tenants. (Unless, of course, it's *your* rental they want to buy. In that case, you may want to structure the deal and look for another property to buy. More about that later...)

MULTI-FAMILY: THE MORE THE MERRIER

When I looked into buying my first rental property, my research showed there was better earning potential in multi-family rather than single family rentals. Throughout this guide, I'm referring to multi-family rentals as buildings with four or less units. Anything above four units is treated as commercial instead of residential housing, and loan terms aren't as favorable for the buyer.

Because I was strapped for cash, the duplex option seemed right for me. For example, if I spent $20,000 on a duplex, two-bedrooms per side, and spent another $10,000 in fix ups, I would have $30,000 in the property, and could earn about $1000 in total rent per month. Using the same figures with a single-family three-bedroom home (you can often find a duplex for the same price as a single-family home), I could earn no more than $700 per month. Although the actual figures will vary in different regions of the U.S., the bottom line will be the same. There's more money to be made in duplexes than single-family homes.

It's interesting to note that if you buy a higher-end duplex for a little more money, the rents you receive don't often reflect that difference. Spending a total of $50,000 on a duplex doesn't mean you're going to be able to charge much higher rent. Be sure to check rents in the area before you buy!

Because income potential was my primary focus, it was pretty much a no-brainer that I'd try my hand at multi-family rentals. However, the process of buying, fixing up and managing rental properties is the same regardless of whether you own single or multi-family homes, so the information contained in this guide will be helpful regardless of which way you go.

To help in your decision-making, it's best to look at your own lifestyle, personality and work situation. Multi-family homes will be more labor-intensive:

- You have two or more tenants and two or more units to repair and manage
- The lease is often month-to-month
- The owner may pay some or all utilities
- Rent is sometimes due on a weekly rather than monthly basis

Time constraints will play a role in your decision. Remember, nothing is written in stone, and you can always jump to the other option if you're not happy with where you are. You've lost nothing as far as your investment goes, and your learning curve will go up regardless of your housing choice. And if you end up hating the whole thing, no problem. My good friend John quit after his first rental. He doesn't have the personality to be a landlord, and he worried about the "what-ifs" all the time. He was driving himself crazy, so he got out. However, he still made money on the sale of his duplex. If you buy smart, you'll make money regardless of whether you buy fifty more, or quit after one.

A quick word here about condos and mobile homes. That word is no. There aren't many low-priced condos out there, and association dues are connected to ownership. The only direction the dues go is up. I'm not a big fan of mobile homes as rentals, because their life span is shorter than other, more permanent homes, and you have to pay a park fee where there are utility hookups. Also, if you live in an area where tornadoes or hurricanes are prevalent, your investment may be here one day and gone the next.

FACE THOSE FEARS

You will encounter challenges if you decide to launch this type of business: analyzing neighborhoods, finding that diamond in the rough, dealing with finances, evicting non-paying tenants and finding good replacements, determining selling strategies, etc. All of these issues will be covered in this book. Whether you choose to invest in single or multi-family units, there's going to be a certain amount of fear and doubt as you begin the journey. First and foremost, don't worry about issues you can't control.

Stress had been my constant companion prior to buying my

first rental. Launching a new career in the midst of personal turmoil overloaded me. I knew from my research that multi-family rentals were my niche, but I was afraid about so many things. Would tenants ruin or vandalize my units? Would there be fights between tenants living next to each other? Would my personality be conducive to landlording? What if I couldn't find reliable tenants? Would the whole thing be more than I could handle, physically and emotionally? Would the plan blow up in my face?

What I've learned is that fear isn't a wall, it's just an emotion. If you walk through it step by step as you approach your goals, it loses its intensity. You may be very uncomfortable for a while, but eventually the fear fades away to nothing.

An excellent remedy for fear is to get in the habit of asking yourself, "Is there anything I can do to change this outcome or remedy this situation?" If the answer is "No" then let it go and move on.

The second remedy for fear is to be prepared. Gather all the information you possibly can. Ask for advice. Quite often, people are too proud to admit they don't know what they're doing. And sure enough, that pride comes back to bite them. My friend Tom has a 30-year-old son who wanted to get into the business. The three of us were at a party together, and Tom asked if I'd be willing to consult with Brad before he got started. I told Brad to give me a call, but he never did. I got the impression he felt very confident about his plan, which is great. Well, he called me two years later, requesting that consulting session. He'd made *numerous* glaring mistakes that could've been prevented had he done his homework, and his investment property had been on the market with no offers for a year and a half. Obviously, Brad hadn't prepared well. Believe me, getting advice from a variety of sources, books, magazines, and other investors will save you a lot of time and money.

THE BOTTOM LINE

Before your first purchase, look at your personality, lifestyle, and work/family commitments. These factors will influence your choice of rental property. Multi-family homes will provide better cash flow than single-family homes, but they're also more labor intensive.

Read about it, and talk with others who've been in the business.

Beware of infomercials and people who boast about the millions they've made and how easy it is. They're exaggerating. I love what I do, but I'm the first to admit you need to be organized and work hard to achieve your goals. Regardless of your past experience or educational background, today's preparation will determine tomorrow's success. Once you've done a couple homes, the process will become somewhat routine; it gets easier with each endeavor.

Truly, the only limits are those you set for yourself. Personal and financial freedom are attainable if you do your homework and stay the course. You're the hero of your own story, as I am of mine. Prepare well, trust yourself, and go for it!

CHAPTER TWO
FINDING THAT GEM OF A DEAL

I FOLLOWED MY REALTOR DOWN the narrow street and parked in front of the nastiest duplex on the block. No problem. Although it needed a facelift on the outside, the roof was fairly new and the aluminum siding was in good shape. After a major cleanup and some minor cosmetics, the outside would look fantastic.

Once inside, we encountered one of the tenants, a surly 300-lb. redhead. He was lounging in a tattered Lazy Boy in his bib overalls with a fat, smoldering stogie clenched between yellowed teeth. My peripheral vision picked up a couple of cockroaches wandering aimlessly across the floor. While my realtor (trying to fit right in) walked casually through the room, Mr. Lazy Boy noticed me eyeing the gun rack on the wall.

"Are you a hunter?" I asked brightly.

"Nah, them're fer perteckshen."

Each house has its pros and cons. This duplex had potential, but the gun rack conversation rattled me a bit. Further research revealed the area had a high incidence of drug-related crimes, so I stopped looking in that neighborhood.

WHERE IS YOUR TARGET AREA?

Legwork, legwork! The real fun begins after deciding which type of property is right for you. First, decide what section of town would be appropriate. For me, the top priority was finding an area no more than 30 minutes from my home. God only knows what gas prices will do, now and in the future. If you plan on buying a bunch of rentals, keep them in the same general area. But make sure the neighborhood's stable and has good growth potential. I bought my first duplex in one neighborhood and when I was unable to find a second bargain there, I sold that one for a fat profit (thank you very much) and targeted a new area. I've been there since. All my rentals are within a three-mile radius of each other.

GETTING INPUT ABOUT THE NEIGHBORHOOD

I suggest spending a good deal of time on this phase. Finding a good area for your rental is of prime importance. This business is income producing, but you're also hoping to build wealth by investing in an area that's going to appreciate in value over the years.

Become familiar with your target area by driving the streets, not just once or twice, but frequently. I visited my potential buying areas several times, and at different times of day. Mornings, midday, evenings, and weekends. This is really the only way to get a feel for the neighborhood you're considering. If you get the chance, stop and speak with residents of the area. They're a wealth of information. Are there many renters in the area? (If the vast majority of homes are rentals, this may lower the stability of the neighborhood.)

Remember Mr. Lazy Boy's neighborhood? After that day, I started checking with the local police department before I wasted my time looking in crime-infested neighborhoods. The criminologist or a detective can provide a printout of how many times they've had to visit the area in the past year, detailing what types of situations were presented. I never worry much about noise violations, domestic disturbance, or neighbors' squabbles. But I'd just as soon keep my distance from murders, gang wars, stabbings and the like. I often work alone, and I don't want to fear for my safety. These occurrences can be hazardous to your health and hazardous to your wealth. Also, you have to assume that at some point down the road, you're going to sell your property, and serious crimes in the area do nothing but drive down property values.

BE A CONSUMER SHOPPER

I love a bargain, whether it's in clothing, food, travel, or investment property. So when I started shopping for rentals, I made my own list of things to look for and things to avoid.

Things to look for:

- The "dog" of the neighborhood. I like to find a decent street with a few homes that have been neglected. These will be good buys.
- Streets where there are more owner-occupied homes than rentals.
- Homes that have brick or vinyl siding. These exteriors are low maintenance.
- Roofs in respectable condition.
- Homes in decent school districts.
- Homes near shopping areas and public transportation.
- Neighborhoods that are growing rather than shrinking. Are new businesses coming into the community? If so, demand for housing will certainly increase. You might check with your local economic development department or the chamber of commerce to find out about growth potential. I bought a property that was west of an urban college campus, after noticing that local business growth was moving in that direction. Not only has the value of my property increased, but also the value of the land underneath.
- Areas where state or federal monies are being used to refurbish old downtown neighborhoods that have seen better days. One of the factors that led me to my investment neighborhood was the amount of renovation going on there. Homes were being re-roofed and sided, and I found out through the police department that my area was part of a national program called "Weed and Seed." Local redevelopment agencies were teaming up with law enforcement to rid the area of run-down, vacant homes, drug problems and other related crimes. I got in on the ground floor, and the neighborhood is progressing slowly but well.

The two homes below are on a typical street, a few doors away from each other. The one that is boarded up is a foreclosure, soon to be auctioned. It will be an excellent buy.

Things to avoid:

- Homes that have already been fixed up. You'll pay more for the property, which decreases your overall profit.
- Homes with wood siding or "insulbrick," which is an asbestos material that simulates the look of brick. Wood exteriors are too much work. Unless you have someone to install vinyl siding at low cost, don't go there. And asbestos is a definite nightmare as far as replacing it and disposing of it in accordance with state and federal regulations.
- Roofs in bad shape that have two or more layers of shingles. Unless you can justify the price of a tear-off and replacement roof in your purchase price, it's not worth it.
- Homes that don't have adequate access to plumbing, heating or electrical boxes. Usually, furnaces and electrical boxes are in plain view. I once bought a duplex that presented a definite plumbing problem. Most of the plumbing for one side of the house was located *under* the floor. The access to it was in the basement crawl space, but that crawl wasn't even big enough for my 105 lb.body. (Not that I would've gone there anyway.......rats, mice, roaches, etc. don't freak me out, but I *am* afraid of spiders. You couldn't pay me enough go into *any* crawl space, large or small.) Anyway, I've since sold that home to another investor. Evidently, the plumbing access issue didn't bother him enough to walk away.
- Monster-size homes. I just got rid of a huge two-bedroom per side duplex that was way too much work. Ten-foot ceilings, room sizes that were too large (17x18 bedrooms, for example) and also a huge yard. It took forever to repaint the rooms, trim out around ceilings, clean up the yard, etc. Too labor intensive. The fact that the home was huge didn't enable me to charge higher rent...it was *still* only two-bedrooms per side.
- Neighborhoods with run-down cars and lots of people hanging out at all hours.
- Houses with porches made of wood. Again, too much work to maintain or replace.
- Neighborhoods posting a multitude of For Rent and For Sale signs. This is not an indication of a healthy real estate market.

- Homes surrounded by businesses. Occasionally, I see a home advertised at a bargain basement price and upon driving by, I understand why it's being sold so cheaply...*no family would want to live there.* If the home doesn't conform to the buildings around it, it's not a bargain.

One more word of advice on finding that gem of an investment... Don't ever be put off by the age of the house. Most of my properties are close to one hundred years old. This *isn't* a bad thing. They're much sturdier than some of the new home construction I see around me every day, and with most of the plumbing, electrical and heat updates having already been completed, these places will be standing long after you and I are gone.

TO REALTOR OR NOT TO REALTOR?

I'm a big proponent of realtors. When I began my rental business, some of my friends and business acquaintances suggested I obtain a realtor's license. Doing so allows you access to the MLS (Multiple Listing Service) and saves money in realtor fees, of course. That route didn't appeal to me, for several reasons. I didn't have the time or money to invest in schooling, and the thought of taking classes and tests just made me tired. I found an excellent realtor who did all the legwork for me. Cheri's reputation for being a great communicator and negotiator was of prime importance to me; her honesty and integrity earned the respect of her clients as well as other realtors.

I did my preliminary research into neighborhoods, but once I'd targeted an area, Cheri took it from there. She gathered "comps" for me, which are listings of all the comparable homes in the area which have sold in the past several months or years. I also had her include all of the current listings. I'd drive by all of them and let her know which ones I wanted to see on the inside. Cheri researched the sale and legal histories of all the homes of interest to me, and took care of many other details that would've taken me hours to cover. I don't have much interest in the "legal schmegal" stuff, and being a realtor involves more of that than you can imagine. I'd rather do all the hands-on things and let someone I trust worry about whether there are liens on the property, whether it has clear title, etc.

Cheri's in the right business for her personality, too. For example, in all the years I've known her, she's never ventured into a basement with me. She's just not a "basement" person (I must admit, some are a little scary) and she's not a "rodent" person either. For example, when we were looking at an abandoned property and I pointed out the decaying mouse in the kitchen sink, she shrieked and performed what came to be known as the mouse dance as she quickly scampered out the front door. She waited there patiently in the yard while I finished inside.

If you enjoy the technical/numbers/legal aspect of your rental business, you may want to pay for the realtor course and obtain your license. You have to go with your personal strengths in this business, and what works for me may not for you. I'm happy to let Cheri do what her expertise allows. She's been kind and patient with me… finding and buying affordable rentals isn't exactly glamorous work, and she's done it with style and finesse. For what she's done for me through the years, Cheri more than deserves her commission as I sell my properties.

BUYING OPPORTUNITIES

In the current real estate market, with foreclosures at an all-time high, there are thousands of cheap single and multi-family homes available. But in a normal real estate market, the smartest time to buy your rental property is in the worst season of the year. Living in Indiana, I try to buy in the dead of winter when I can. No one puts a house on the market in December or January unless they absolutely have to get rid of it. Figure out which season will be a buyer's market in your area, and try to buy during that time.

There are many ways in which you may acquire your rental properties. Driving through your chosen neighborhood will show you most of them.

1) **Homes for sale through realty companies.** The majority of homes (85%) will be sold this way. I've bought most of my properties this way. I usually call the phone number on the yard

sign for preliminary information; my realtor sets up a showing if I'm interested in looking inside.

2) **Tax and Sheriff Sales.** Tax Sales are usually held once or twice a year, and are mainly comprised of homes that were taken from their owners because they hadn't paid property taxes for a prolonged period of time. Each county conducts these sales differently, but you can call the Auditor's office to obtain information. The office will provide you with a list of properties to be sold, along with the addresses. You aren't allowed access to the inside of the dwelling, which is a disadvantage, but you can sometimes tell a lot by looking at the outside and peeking in the windows. The sale is run like an auction, and the bidding starts with the amount in back property taxes owed on the home. For example, if the homeowner is in arrears to the amount of $4000, that's where the bidding begins. There are definitely bargains to be had here! However, if you win the bid, you receive a certificate that has to be held by you for a period of three months to two years, in which time the homeowner has the right to buy it back from the city if he can manage to pay the back taxes. So, you have to be willing to wait it out. (I'm not willing.) When you officially take ownership of the property, the city assures that there are no liens on the property and the title is free and clear, which is a nice advantage to this type of purchase. Check with your local Auditor's office to obtain information. Sheriff's Sales are a little different. They contain houses that have been repossessed because the mortgage hasn't been paid, or because a creditor has taken the house to satisfy a debt. You can call the local Sheriff's office to find out how often these are held. In my area, these sales are held once a month, and there are homes in a wide variety of price ranges. When interest rates are low, people are tempted to purchase a more expensive home than they can truly afford. They may acquire a big home with the accompanying big fat mortgage. If they lose their job or some other financial hardship happens, they can't pay the mortgage and they lose the house. And that's where we come in. Over the past few years, foreclosures have been commonplace throughout the country; there are at least 500 properties that show up in my local sale each month. In the

Sheriff's Sale, the bidding price begins with the judgment amount, or what was owed on the mortgage; there are mortgage amounts ranging from the low thousands all the way up into hundreds of thousands. As with the tax sale, you don't have the opportunity to get inside the house, but if you buy a property at the Sheriff's Sale, you get possession within a few days. Both types of sales include a wide range of dwellings, and I've watched investors purchase 50 or 100 at a time. When they officially become the owners of the property, many of them are willing to resell a few to people like me. They may tack a few thousand onto the price, but even at that it's still a good deal.

3) **Foreclosures.** The Sheriff Sale handles foreclosures, but many of them are also listed through realty companies. They've gotten these listings from banks or mortgage companies, neither of whom wants to own real estate. Throughout 2008-10, many borrowers who lost their homes actually owed more on them than the home was worth; the banks and mortgage companies have had to take the loss. I've bought several foreclosed homes. Many of them have been vacant for awhile (like the mouse-in-the-sink house) and have had all the utilities turned off, which makes it a difficult to check whether everything's in working order. However, if the electrical boxes and furnace/water heater look decent, you can assume the potential problems are minor. Check with someone in the foreclosure office of a bank or lending company to find out about foreclosures. If you can get your foot in the door with a lender, you may be able to receive advance notice of foreclosures in your area. Many foreclosures don't make it to the real estate listings because someone like you or me has an "in," and snaps them up before they reach the open market. A realtor can also help you find foreclosures.

4) **FSBO** (For Sale by Owner). You can find these when you're driving the streets of your chosen neighborhood, or sometimes by talking to homeowners in the area. Maybe grandma, two doors down, has just died, and her kids want to unload the house. Or maybe the young couple next door has been laid off and can't pay their mortgage, and they need a way out. I just bought a nice little house from an 81-year-old guy who had a tiny handwritten sign

in his yard. We now have a good working relationship and he's put me onto another house down the street that someone wants to sell. It's amazing what you can learn by talking to people in the neighborhood. And, if they see that you fix up your homes nicely and rent them to decent people, they'll be happy to see you buy another and another, because it improves the resale value of their own home. This is a no-hassle way to buy, if the current owner has all the appropriate paperwork in line. If you take this opportunity, you may want to have a real estate attorney or your realtor go over everything before you sign papers.

5) **Auctions**. This option represents an excellent opportunity to pick up housing at under-market prices. After seeing a realty company for sale sign in the yard, I bought a duplex for $35,000. A mortgage company had tried to sell the house at auction a few weeks before. The top bid at the auction was $20,000, so they decided to put it on the market in hopes of getting more money for it. Had I known about the auction, I might have been able to pick it up for $25-30,000. These homes come from estates, foreclosures and a variety of other situations. You never know who's going to show up at an auction. I do my homework before I attend. I know the value of the surrounding properties and what I'm willing to spend. You're usually required to pay (certified) 10% of the price that day, with the remaining funds paid within a month or so. It varies. Sometimes you can buy cheap at an auction, and other times you'll see a property sell for more than it's worth. Real estate auctions are advertised in the local newspaper, or through a sign in the yard. You can also contact local auction houses and have them notify you of upcoming auction sales.

6) **University Housing**. This type of rental property consists of any home that's close enough to a college or university to be desirable housing for students. If you can find a single or multi-family home that's within your price range, buy it! If there's a housing shortage at the college, rentals in the area are going to be in high demand. Back in 1998, when my daughter Allison was attending Ball State University, I put an offer on a four-bedroom two-story home. The plan was for her and some friends to live there, and she would be

my mini-manager. I offered a couple thousand below full price, and someone beat me to it. Hind sight tells me I should've offered full price, because I would've been nicely compensated in the astronomical rents I could've asked and gotten. I currently manage two rentals near Butler University, and whereas I could get $800/month for the same house in another area of Indianapolis, I'm pulling $1400/month for each of these properties. Although I'm not the owner of the properties, the management income (12% of rents) is a nice supplement to my income from my own properties. Can you put up with the possible antics and hassles associated with renting to college kids? If so, then buy university housing if you get the chance.

7) **Other Investors' Homes**. With a little networking, which I'll discuss in the next chapter, you can find great deals from other people like you. For example, my friend Tom sold me the duplex below duplex for $10,000 because he'd gotten it for less than that at the tax sale and didn't really want to keep it for his own portfolio. Initially, it was a shell of a house, inside and out. A new roof and vinyl siding transformed the exterior in less than a week. I had to put $15,000 into it, but could easily sell it for $60,000 today, and I've made good rental income in the six years I've owned it.

DO-IT-YOURSELF INSPECTIONS

When you find a property that appeals to you, it's time to thoroughly check it out. Many investors submit their offer, and include in that offer their intention to have an official home inspection performed by an outside company. The offer is contingent upon the buyer accepting the inspection findings, or working it out with the seller to complete some repairs (at the seller's expense) that have been pointed out in the inspection.

You need to realize at this point that any official inspection performed is going to yield pages and pages of defects in the house. Some of those defects are very minute and could easily be found in your house or mine; others are significant enough to be deal breakers if the owner isn't willing to negotiate on the repair, or lower the price of the house. If the seller is motivated and wants to get rid of his property quickly, he may agree to pay for several of the items mentioned in the inspection report. I would highly recommend obtaining your own estimates for repairs, so that you can feel assured that the work will be done correctly. Sometimes, when the seller offers to have "his people" do the work, you find out later that "his people" were idiots who totally screwed up the job.

Because I was a little nervous about the whole process of buying rentals, I involved a home inspection company in my first two or three purchases. It was worth the price (a few hundred each) for my peace of mind. Ask a dependable realtor to a recommend a reputable home inspection company; realtors talk amongst themselves and can tell you where to go for a high quality inspection at a reasonable price.

Within a few years, I learned that if I could perform my own inspection, and state in my offer that I was *not* requiring an inspection, that concession would sway the sellers. Foregoing the official inspection is a nice little perk to offer the seller, because it eliminates the often long, drawn out process of going back and forth with the buyer regarding what the sellers are willing to fix and what they aren't. If you can combine that tactic with a cash offer, the seller may accept a discounted sale price. I've been on both ends of the deal, and I know it works for both buyers and sellers.

Okay, so let's look at foregoing the inspection and doing it yourself. Where do you start? I'd looked at numerous houses after a couple years of being in this business, and had developed a pretty good eye for what defects were minimal and what defects were deal breakers. Also, I'd found a very good handyman who was helping me with my rentals, and for his usual hourly fee, I used him as my informal inspector. I saved hundreds of dollars this way.

Any major defects you find should be seriously considered:

- Furnaces that are ancient or inoperable
- Foundations that are crumbling, causing the house to lean
- Roofs and siding in bad shape
- Electrical boxes and wiring that are so old and tangled they look downright scary

You may want to get quotes on these repairs beforehand so that you can take the cost into consideration when you make an offer. Most properties in the low price ranges will contain many defects; the above list includes potential deal breakers, while the list below is pretty much par for the course:

- Windows that are broken, or missing storm windows
- Filthy, smelly carpet, old vinyl or tile flooring
- Cracks and chunks of wall that are missing
- Toilets, sinks, and appliances that are missing or disgustingly dirty
- Critter infestations (mice, rats, roaches, nasty tenants)

Although these problems may exist, they don't require huge amounts of money in fix ups, particularly if you plan on doing a majority of the work yourself. I'll get to that fun fix-up stuff later.

THE BOTTOM LINE

Finding a good area for your rental is essential. This business will make money for you now, but you're also hoping to build wealth by investing in an area that will appreciate in value as the years go by. Do your homework and pick an area that's showing signs of improvement.

Once you target your neighborhood, scout out that diamond in the rough. There are many ways to buy, with or without a realtor. Educate yourself about various government sales and other buying opportunities, and be ready to move quickly when an opportunity presents itself. Of course, to move quickly, you'll need to have your financing figured out ahead of time, which leads us to the following chapter...

CHAPTER THREE

FINANCING...THE "F" WORD

OKAY, SO I GUESS we all know how I feel about financing and the world of calculations and math. I'm not a numbers cruncher by nature, having struggled miserably through Algebra and Geometry as a kid. If you have a math mind, working on this portion of investing will be something you enjoy. For me, it's a necessary evil. With that said, I've found it doesn't have to be confusing if you rely on others' expertise. Networking with my accountant, realtor and other investors has helped eliminate my discomfort and confusion regarding financing.

FIGURE IT OUT BEFOREHAND!

The main thing you need to know before you make an offer is this: how am I going to finance this deal? You might want to take a good hard look at your spending habits. Have you checked your credit rating lately? You may do so at www.annualcreditreport.com (877-322-8228). Are you carrying high balances on your credit cards, or do you pay them off monthly? Are you an impulse shopper? Do you indulge in expensive toys you could do without? Do you really need that boat? Motorcycle? Second or third car? Fancy clothes, shoes, mocha lattes, sculptured nails, iPods, iPhones, electronic toys, etc.? You may want to consider selling the non-essentials, and trimming back on your debt. This strategy will put more money in your pocket and improve your overall financial big picture. A little self-sacrifice won't kill you. Unlike me, you probably have the luxury of planning this adventure ahead of time. Patience, planning and self-discipline will serve you well.

Even though lenders have tightened their purse strings since 2008, they are still willing to help you with a purchase if you have good credit; when I launched my real estate investing career, I had *no* credit. While I was married, it didn't occur to me to have credit cards or other accounts in my name alone; I didn't establish a separate credit identity for myself. So when everything fell apart, legitimate lenders avoided me like the plague. (Can't say I blame them…) In those early years, I was forced to be creative with my financing.

As you're determining your target area, you should also be researching your options for financing. You need to know, going in, *what* you can pay for the property, and *how* you're going to pay for it. When these things have been figured out, you're ready to roll.

CASH DEALS

When I bought my first rental, I used monies I'd received from my divorce. That first duplex cost me $19,000, and the purchase moved quickly because I was paying cash for the home. Like I said in the last chapter, sellers love it when someone offers cash for their property, because they know there won't be any glitches with the buyer's ability to pay. They're often willing to come down on their asking price if you're:

1) paying cash
2) willing to forego an official inspection
3) willing to close the deal quickly

If you can structure this kind of deal, you'll be amazed at the incredible bargains to be had. This is called "making money going in," when you're able to buy below market value. If the average home in the area sells for $50,000, and you can buy one for $25,000, put in $10,000 for fix ups, ending up with a total of $35,000 invested, then you've made $15,000 up front! If you're thorough in researching your target area, you know market values, and proceed as described above, you'll make thousands of dollars going in.

I spent $8,000 fixing up my first duplex, which I'd bought for $19,000. After renting it for a little over a year, I decided it might be time to add another rental. I had found the work challenging and interesting, and felt my personality was conducive to being a landlord. Unfortunately, there were no other great deals in that neighborhood. I had to look elsewhere; I researched three other neighborhoods before settling on my new target area, which has become my "final resting place" including eight duplexes, two triplexes, one four-plex, and three single-family homes…a grand total of twenty-nine units. I affectionately call it "the hood;" it's become as familiar to me as my own neighborhood.

Having done my homework prior to buying that first rental, I'd made money going in when I paid a very low price for it. I put a total of $27,000 into that home, listed it through my realtor at $43,000 and received a full price offer the first day it was on the market. And then kicked myself for not putting a higher price tag on it. Hindsight's 20/20. Anyway, profits from that sale were quickly used to purchase my second duplex. After buying and fixing it up for a total of $30,000, I wanted to continue my path, but money was tight. A home equity credit line enabled me to keep building my rental portfolio.

HOME EQUITY CREDIT LINES

Because I had equity in my own home, I was able to obtain a credit line against that equity. Many banks offer this type of loan, and interest rates are competitive. This financing technique is as effective as cash, because it's quick and simple. No hassle. You write a certified check out of the account to purchase a property, then pay the account back on a monthly basis, like you would any other loan. While building my business, I made interest only payments; the interest on my account was prime plus a half percent, which was very good at the time. Since then, I've increased the amount of the credit line by $45,000, and my current rate is prime plus a quarter percent. Home equity lines are very common, and if you own part or all of your personal dwelling, buying with a home equity account is an easy way to add to your rental portfolio. Just be sure you're willing to make that monthly payment; your own home is at stake here.

MORTGAGES

Of course, you can always go the route of the traditional mortgage, although this is always a fluctuating situation, dependent on the economy. Banks and mortgage brokers offer all types of mortgage opportunities. I prefer mortgage brokers, simply because they'll shop around for the best deal. My realtor was able to provide me with names of several reliable brokers with whom she'd done business over the years.

The beauty of mortgages is that you can build your real estate portfolio without investing huge amounts of money in one property. With my initial $19,000, which I paid in cash for a duplex, I could've taken out mortgages on two separate properties, putting $10,000 down on one and $9,000 down on another. But like I said, mortgage companies avoided me like the plague (the credit issue) so it wasn't an option. If your credit's in decent shape, the mortgage option might be a good way to go. Most lenders will demand 20% down on an investment property, but occasionally they'll take less and allow you to take out a second mortgage for the rest.

One downfall to the traditional mortgage is the time required to put it in place, i.e. qualifying, etc. Getting pre-approved will help expedite the process. The seller, knowing you have pre-approval, will be more willing to seriously consider your offer. Another disadvantage to mortgages is that companies charge higher interest rates on mortgages for investment properties. For example, my mortgage company charged me nine percent interest, in 1997, on a loan that would have cost me six percent if it had been for my personal dwelling. Now, you *can* avoid the higher rates if you plan to live in the property for a couple years. I know people who bought a duplex as their first rental property and lived in half of it so they could qualify for the lower interest rate. They rented out the other half and paid the mortgage with the rental income. Sweet deal, huh? After the required period of time passed, they bought another property and did the same thing. This plan works well for those who don't have personal situations or responsibilities that tie them to one particular house. Interest rates also vary according to how much money you give as a down payment. Putting more money down may improve your interest rate.

If you decide to obtain a mortgage, you'll need to make sure the rents you receive from the property will more than cover the cost of your monthly mortgage payment, taxes and insurance. Remember, if your rental stands empty for awhile, or if your tenant stops paying rent for one reason or another, that mortgage payment still looks you in the face. Never assume you're going to have 100% occupancy. It just doesn't happen.

Also, if you secure a mortgage, make sure you won't be penalized for paying down on the mortgage before the loan term (15, 30 years, or whatever) has expired. My mortgages contain no pre-payment penalties, and I pay down on the principle amounts every chance I get.

I took advantage of this financing method *after* I'd bought four properties. I took out mortgages on two of the properties after I'd fixed them up. One of the homes had been bought for $24,000, and my total investment after fix up was $32,000. The mortgage company required an appraisal that would help them determine the value of the property. The house in question appraised at $50,000; my $8,000 in fix ups turned into an appraisal that was $18,000 more than I'd invested in the property. The other home performed just as well, and the cash I received at the closing of these two mortgages enabled me to buy two more properties.

Sometimes it's possible to take over the seller's loan when you buy his property. This is called an assumable loan, and although I've never had the opportunity to buy this way, assuming the loan cuts out a lot of the red tape associated with buying the property. Assuming a loan can save you money if the interest rate on the seller's mortgage is lower than the current rate.

PRIVATE LOANS----LET'S BE CREATIVE

Private loans are a wonderful way to get financing, if you're careful about with whom you deal. Sometimes, depending on his/her financial situation, the current owner of a property may be willing to "carry back" the loan, which is another term for seller financing. The seller agrees to finance the property, often with a small down payment as well as a reasonable interest rate. This method simplifies the sale and eliminates fees. Family and personal friends are definite options for providing private loans, but everything rests on both parties being comfortable with the provisions of the loan.

I've had people willing to lend me money, in return for a piece of the action. No way! I want to avoid sharing the profits of my hard work if I can. Does that make me a greedy little moneymonger? No, just a smart businessperson. In addition, I've heard too many horror stories about various partnerships going awry, resulting in substantial attorney fees and court costs. I try to keep life simple. Close friends have been willing to loan me money at no interest, but even if you have to pay some interest on the loan, it's simpler than obtaining a traditional bank loan.

Don't rule out the possibility of borrowing from other investors, either. I know several people who've been real estate investors for many years, and they've moved from buying, fixing up and managing like I do, to simply being the bank for investors like me. Most of their borrowers (other investors) do short-term loans; they'll buy a property with the loaned money, fix it up, and get a mortgage on it as soon as possible. They use the cash received at the mortgage closing to repay the initial loan. Because these investors who act as the bank charge a hefty interest rate, sometimes 14 to 18 percent, it makes sense to use their money only on a short-term basis.

Needless to say, trust is a key factor when you use other individuals for financing, but it may be an easy, effective way to create more opportunities for yourself. As with every aspect of this business, you'll determine what suits your own personality when it comes to financing. Keeping it simple works for me; I don't like debt, and my primary goal is to decrease debt and improve the assets I have. Your real estate investment goals will drive most of your decisions. My eye is always on the long-term goal of owning all my properties free and clear, and I've tried to tailor my financing to that goal.

THE BOTTOM LINE

Figuring out your financing ahead of time will help you get the best deal possible. Know how much you're able to spend and get everything in place *before* you make an offer. Sellers love cash deals and will consider a low offer rather than wait it out with a buyer who's trying to qualify for a loan. If you decide to go the mortgage route, get pre-approval before submitting offers. This will show that you're a legitimate buyer.

The decision to use cash, a home equity credit line, mortgage, or a personal loan will be driven by your financial situation, personality and investment goals. Above all, you must know the deal will bring good cash flow. I use a simple worksheet that provides me that answer, and I'll share it with you in the following chapter.

CHAPTER FOUR

GO AHEAD, MAKE AN OFFER

YOU'VE EARMARKED A PROPERTY that makes sense for you to buy, and you've either hired a home inspection company or have done your own assessment on the condition of the property and what it will take, in time and money, to fix it up.

CHECK THE NUMBERS BEFORE YOU BUY

There's one more tool I've used to estimate the short- and long-term money-making value of the rental property, and I always cross check my own research with this particular worksheet. It's an excellent tool to use along with your own research methods, and I'm including it on the following page.

DIAMOND OR DUD?

Before you put an offer on a property, fill out this worksheet to figure out if it's worth buying. Number 10 is an important number. This is the amount of money in your pocket after all expenses each year.

Number 11 will give you the annual return you can expect on the cash you invest, once the property is in rentable condition. If that number is above 10%, go for it.

Note: All the figures below should be in annual amounts.

1. Rental Income	
Subtract 5% for vacancy and uncollected rents	
2. This total (rents minus 5%) is your net rent	
3. Deductible expenses:	
Repairs (10% of rental income, #1)	
Property taxes	
Insurance	
Management fees	
Utilities: Electricity	
Gas	
Water	
Total deductible expenses	
4. Net operating income before mortgage expense	
Subtract #3 from #2	
5. Mortgage payment	
6. Pre-tax cash flow: subtract #5 from #4	
7. Depreciation: what you paid for the building ÷ 27.5 years	
8. Tax loss or gain: Subtract #7 from #6	
9. Tax loss or tax due: Multiply #8 by your % tax bracket	
10. After tax cash flow: #6 plus or minus #9	
11. Cash-on-cash return: #10 ÷ the cash invested (cost plus fix ups)	

I've never been super-interested in the stock market, although I do have some investments through a financial planner. With the market, it's not easy to get ten percent or more return on your investment. But real estate, if you buy it right, fix it up, and manage it well, can produce a safe, steady return of ten percent and more. I've had a couple properties dip down below that level for one reason or another (i.e. a big jump in property tax, higher than normal vacancy rates, etc.) and I've sold them and moved on to something more profitable. My four-plex yields at least a 26% return on my investment *every* year. I call it the cash cow. Can you get that kind of return consistently in the market?

If you have questions about some of the info in this worksheet, your accountant can easily clear up any confusion you might have. Using this tool serves to justify my research and gut feeling about buying a property. It's my seal of approval prior to submitting my offer and I highly recommend it to all. If my target property doesn't meet the requirements in the worksheet, I walk away regardless of how enamored I was with the property. You can't make emotional decisions, and the numbers in the worksheet don't lie.

Most of the homes I've bought were empty when I put in the offer. If there are tenants in the home, you'll need to decide whether or not you want to let them stay past the term of their lease. Most places need at least some updating, and you may want to get the current tenants out. If so, check with the sellers regarding the current lease stipulations. You should be given a copy of the lease at the closing. If you plan to let them stay but are intending to raise the rent, you'll need to let them know in writing. It's best to go to the house and introduce yourself; I'd give them a letter with all your contact numbers, and include a copy of the new lease for their perusal. They may decide to move; give them a time frame in which they need to get back with you regarding their decision.

I bought a duplex once that was occupied by two elderly couples. The rents there were ridiculously low, and I had every intention of raising them immediately. After meeting with them a couple times, I just didn't have the heart to do it. They were sweet people, on very limited incomes, had lived there for over twenty years, and couldn't afford to pay more rent. So I let things be, and after a couple years,

I sold the place. Fortunately, I made good money on the sale. I still visit one of the old ladies, who resides in a senior citizens' apartment building. The moral of the story? If you're too softhearted to make the right financial decision after buying, don't buy in the first place.

When I find a property that's a real gem, I try to make the offer as quickly as possible; there are other investors out there with whom I'm competing, and they've beaten me to the punch on a couple of occasions. So, my advice is to jump on it and get the offer in quickly.

If you've figured out your financing and have done your own inspection and research, you're ready to hit the seller with a deal he can't refuse. The county clerk at your local courthouse can help you find out what the previous purchase price was and what the mortgage amount is on the property. (Sellers will rarely accept an offer that's below their mortgage amount.) If you're using a realtor, he/she can also help you find out some past history on the house. Offer cash or be pre-approved for a mortgage, forego the official inspection, and be ready to close the following week. I always offer much less than the asking price; if your first offer is accepted, you've gone in too high. Expect a counter offer, and just be sure you know what is the highest price you're willing to pay. This is particularly important if you're buying in an auction setting. I've seen homes be stolen at auctions, but I've also seen them be sold at higher than market value, due to buyers getting in bidding wars and being swept away by the competitive spirit that exists at auctions.

THE BOTTOM LINE

Do your homework. Know the neighborhood values, get a good ballpark figure on what you'll need to spend in fix ups, arrange for financing, and fill out the worksheet included in this chapter. If the worksheet gives you good feedback, you're ready to make the offer. Move quickly, with intention to close quickly.

Always come in with a low offer, know the top amount you're willing to pay, and be willing to walk away if you're tempted to pay more than you know it's worth. There are plenty of properties out there and another will come along.

CHAPTER FIVE
INSURANCE AND LIABILITY

SHOP AROUND

IF YOU'RE WILLING TO bet that no catastrophe will ever happen at one of your properties…no fires, no vandalism, no storm damage, no irate tenant hell bent on suing you for millions, then feel free to skip this chapter. But before you do, let me tell you a little story…

I've filed only one claim in my career, but it was rather major, to say the least. Late one afternoon, as I sat sipping a glass of wine with my friend Jan, my pager went off. I wore my pager all the time, because being available to my tenants is of prime importance to me. This was before I got the cell phone and tossed the pager. I had a couple tenants who always paged me with a "911" after their number, which in the beginning totally freaked me out. When I called their number in response to the page, they'd ask me something like, "Can I paint my bathroom black?" So when I got this page I turned to Jan and said jokingly, "Gee, a page with 911 after it. Someone must have a light bulb burned out."

When I called the number, Jeannie, who lives next door to one of my rentals, was *screaming* over the sirens in the background.

"Barb! It's Jeannie! Your house is on fire! The whole street's blocked off!"

I told her I'd be there in a half hour, turned to Jan and said, "Gotta go…one of my rentals is on fire."

By the time I got there the fire was out, but half the duplex was totally destroyed. The fire chief approached me and said it looked like an old overturned space heater had started the fire. Interestingly enough, I'd just filed eviction on the nineteen-year-old guy that lived in that apartment. The neighbor said she'd seen him earlier in the day, but after the fire, I never heard from that kid again. Although I was evicting him, our relationship had been pleasant; I can't imagine the fire was intentionally set. It's a mystery, but I'm so grateful the house was insured.

Although I'm always the optimist, even *I'm* smart enough to know I'd best cover my properties and myself in the event disaster strikes. I'd advise you to read this chapter carefully.

One of the first items on my list when adding a property to my portfolio is securing an insurance policy on the home. Always the consumer shopper, I've chosen to go with an independent agent who will shop around and find me the best coverage for the lowest price. I have all of my insurance (personal dwelling, autos, health and rental properties) with him; the savings on premiums are significant when you get everything through one agent.

The first issue to address is this: What should the value of the insurance policy be? Should the dollar amount be equal to the market value of the home, or should it be for the amount of money it would take to rebuild the home if it burned to the ground? (This is called replacement value.) I discussed this at length with my agent Bob. With building costs constantly on the rise, we determined it might cost $80,000 to replace a property that was a $40,000 investment, including sale price and fix ups. If I rebuilt for $80,000, that house would stick out like a sore thumb; the neighborhood's nicest home would sell for $60,000. It didn't make sense to pay the higher premium, knowing I wouldn't rebuild the house in the event of a total loss. I'd just take the money and run. And buy two more.

We decided it was smarter to insure the home for what I felt was the current market value, or for the amount of money I had invested in the house. My $40,000 home could be sold for $50,000, so I set the policy value at $50,000, which provided adequate coverage at a low price. A few years down the road, as neighborhood vales went up, I just upped the value another $10,000.

To help keep my premiums low, my deductible amount is $1,000. So with any claim I might file, the first $1,000 in repair is mine to pay, and the insurance company takes it from there. Some companies are a bit skittish about insuring rental properties, so to keep them from raising my rates or dropping me altogether, I don't file insignificant claims. Also, I pay my premiums once a year instead of quarterly or monthly, avoiding the service charge they may add if they bill more frequently.

When the insurance company sends someone out to check the home, they'll give you a list of items that need to be addressed within a certain time period. For example, concrete steps that are crumbling, four or more outdoor steps with no handrail, holes in the yard, etc. When you do your initial fix ups, reduce your exposure to tenant injuries on your property by taking care of these issues. The inspector from the insurance company doesn't go inside, because the agent asks a series of questions about the interior when you fill out the application. It's important that the heat, electrical, and roof have been replaced or updated.

One of the homes I bought had a lot of potential, but the garage in back was a total eyesore. I was curious as to how the insurance people would react and sure enough, the company took issue with it. The garage was very old, the wood was a little rotten in several spots, and the roof was in pretty bad shape, too. In other words, it was a disaster waiting to happen. I just had them exclude the garage in my coverage. If it burned down or got blown away, I'd consider it a blessing. I eventually had the garage torn down.

If you do a decent job of fixing up the home, there just isn't much that can go wrong. Of course, you'll have the normal, minor disasters such as furnaces going out, water heaters rusting out the bottom and flooding the area, etc., but these aren't big enough losses to file claims, especially if your deductible is high.

I'd like to get back to the fire story for a moment. That fire burned the first and second floor of one apartment, which had to be rebuilt from scratch, beginning with new floors, studs and ceilings. I went down there the following day with my camera, not because I thought my insurance company wouldn't take care of me, but because I was curious and wanted pictures for myself. It was a bright sunny day, but the inside was totally black with soot, so it was pretty dark in there. Two of the steps leading to the second floor were completely burned out, but I confidently stepped over the abyss (which was open to the basement) and ventured upstairs with my camera.

After taking a few pictures, I began the tricky descent. Unfortunately,

I misjudged the location of the burned out steps, and stepped right into the gaping hole. My hips slammed into the edge of the opening and my hands hit hard in a pile of rubble at the base of the stairway. Legs dangling down into the hole, totally pissed off at my own stupidity, I uttered a few choice words and pulled myself out. My hands were filthy and bleeding, and one of the lenses in my glasses had popped out in the freefall. One of the cuts in my hand was deep enough to require a trip to the local hand surgeon, who had to dig a bunch of junk out of it before pulling it together. Lovely. This incident is a classic example of what I call a "dumbass attack." I've suffered hundreds of these attacks throughout my real estate investing career, but have learned from each of them.

The moral of the story? Overconfidence is an accident waiting to happen. I had no business going in there in the first place. If you sustain structural damage to an apartment, stay out!

The good news resulting from that fire is my insurance took good care of me. I had $32,000 in the house, and insured it for $45,000. The damage to that *one* apartment totaled $38,000. When everything was finished, the apartment looked beautiful. I painted the interior in exchange for paying my $1,000 deductible, so when it was all said and done, no money left my pocket. Although I wouldn't wish any misfortune on my properties, it's comforting to know things will be taken care of if, indeed, a tragedy occurs. The pictures below are before and after shots of the rebuild following the fire.

WATCH YOUR BACK!

I initially set up my business as a sole proprietorship, because it was the easiest and cheapest avenue for me, although not the smartest choice in regard to liability and privacy. This and other business options will be discussed in the chapter on accounting. I mention it here because as a sole proprietor, the easiest way to cover yourself for liability is through an umbrella policy attached to your homeowner's insurance. My umbrella policy was in addition to the liability portion included in my insurance for each rental. For each of my properties, the policy covered me for $500,000 in liability. Bob recommended I insure myself for a million dollars over and above the amounts contained in the rentals' policies. That million-dollar umbrella is cheap, under $200/year, and more than worth it for the peace of mind it provided.

I believe there are two reasons I've never been sued or even threatened with a lawsuit:

1) My apartments and yards are very well maintained. Stairways, sidewalks, etc. are what they call "to code," which means they meet the requirements set by the city's safe housing department. Smoke alarms are present on every floor, and also the basement. Some states require carbon monoxide detectors, fire extinguishers, etc. Check on these issues with your agent. The electrical and other systems are updated. If you're remiss in any of these areas and someone gets injured on your property, good luck! I *have* had tenants and/or their friends get hurt (not seriously) on my property, but fortunately, they realize they were at fault.

2) My tenants respect me. This is every bit as important as number (1). Think about it. If you neglect your apartments and are nasty, inattentive and condescending to your tenants, they'll resent and dislike you. If the opportunity arises, they'll happily sue you. On the other hand, if your tenants see you working hard and taking good care of the property, they'll respect your efforts and appreciate you. Tenants are never inclined to sue a landlord who treats them fairly.

Take the above advice seriously. If you do, your chances of getting sued will be slim to none.

THE BOTTOM LINE

Chances are, no major catastrophes will befall your rentals. But you can't take that chance. As soon as you close on a property, secure a good insurance policy. I use a broker, who shops around for the best prices. It makes sense to insure the properties for the current market value, rather than replacement value. Having all my policies (health, autos, personal dwelling and rentals) with one agent has resulted in savings across the board.

Keeping your rentals in good condition and treating your tenants with kindness and respect will minimize your chances of being sued. But a good, solid insurance policy guarantees peace of mind.

CHAPTER SIX
GOT IT! (NOW WHAT??)

YOU'RE THE PROUD OWNER of a dump with tremendous potential. If you've planned and executed efficiently, you'll be ready to get started immediately after you close on the property.

You'll feel overwhelmed as you tackle your first rehabbing job. If you break it down into small segments like I've done in this chapter, it'll feel more manageable. After you've done a couple units, the fix-up process will be routine. As you move through the fix-up, be aware of what the surrounding properties look like inside. Check out the other rentals in the area by peeking in the windows, attending open houses, or setting up an appointment to see them; you could be looking on behalf of an imaginary relative. When you do your own renovations, it's important that you measure up to your competition. If you don't, you rental will stand empty.

As you begin the rehab process, remember that you must view your rental neighborhood and tenants' lives differently than you do your own. This may seem obvious, but many first-time investors make the mistake of meshing the two. Your goal is to get it up and running as quickly as possible and have it compare favorably with other homes in the area. The tendency is to overdo it on the rehab and include bells and whistles similar to what we'd include in our own homes...things that run up the rehab bill, but won't bring in higher rents.

As the new property owner, you'll have a packet of paperwork you received at the closing. I keep an ownership file on each of my properties, which includes everything from the closing: the listing sheet, purchase offers, loan documents, insurance policies, home inspection, deed, etc. It's wise to keep these important documents in a fireproof filing cabinet.

Except for the property with the two sweet elderly couples, all the properties I've purchased have been vacant when I took possession. Remember, if there are tenants in the home, you'll be required to enforce the terms of their current lease throughout its duration. If you're planning on redoing the inside, you'll need to inform the tenant, verbally and in writing, that the lease will not be renewed at the end of its term. You will have been given a copy of the lease at closing. Read through it carefully to ensure the tenant hasn't been promised anything outlandish, such as all new flooring, appliances or other expensive upgrades after a specified time period. You may want to send the current tenants a letter, introducing yourself as the new landlord. You can include a "Tenant Information Sheet," in which you'll ask for all the occupants' names, ages, contact numbers for home and work, emergency contact numbers, Social Security numbers and dates of birth. You can tell them you need this information for your rental files, and supply a self-addressed, stamped envelope.

After getting possession of the property, the first thing I do is take photographs of the home, both inside and outside. These before pictures are great reminders of the total transformation that takes place at the house. I enjoy looking back at those photographs, even years after the purchase.

Do you need to buy a vehicle to be used exclusively for work? Not at all. I owned a 1995 Toyota Corolla when I began my career. It had to double as my work vehicle. There was no extra money to purchase a used truck or work car, so I did what I had to do. The inside of the car got trashed a few times, like the day I failed to put a paint can lid on tightly, and a half gallon of dark brown paint leaked all over my light gray fabric interior. Or, the day I'd been using an extremely toxic chemical to clear a sink drain. Again, a lid that was slightly ajar. By the time I got home, some of the spilled acid had eaten a huge hole in the back seat fabric; I could see right down to the steel frame. I don't use scary chemicals anymore; I make a call to my plumber. But, I still have that little Corolla, which is now just my work vehicle, and has close to 200,000 miles on the odometer. My trunk is packed to the hilt with all kinds of stuff, and so is the back seat. But everything I need on a regular basis is at my fingertips, and that little car has been a great work vehicle. A few of my houses have garages, and I use one of them for storing larger items. My handyman also uses the garage for some of his things; he's got some pack rat tendencies though, and sometimes I have to tell him to trim down the contents.

After you become the owner of your new property, load up your car or truck and get started. Remember, every day that passes is a day on which you're not getting any rent money, so get on it!

FIND HELP

Hopefully, you've secured a reliable, honest handyman who has the time and energy to help you with the rehabbing process. Many cities have free newspapers that advertise repair people of all kinds. Some of them have full-time jobs, but like to do side work to earn extra money. For the most part, they don't charge an arm and a leg for the work, and I've had excellent luck finding workers this way. When I mention that I have several properties to a potential repairman, he'll often quote me a very reasonable rate, knowing there's an opportunity for many repair jobs within my business. Networking with friends, other investors or even your realtor are other avenues for finding good help. I joined the local landlord association and have gotten many referrals for all kinds of repair people from members of this group.

For my first couple of rentals, I used a small maintenance company; I'd found them through another investor. The two guys who did the bulk of the work were knowledgeable and willing to share their expertise. My learning curve skyrocketed as I worked alongside them. Quickly, my motto became, "Don't pay anyone to do something you can do yourself." Every repair you do on your own saves you money. There are several home repair books on the market. *Dare to Repair*, by Sussman and Glakas-Tenet, *Reader's Digest Fix It Yourself Manual*, and *Home Improvement for Dummies* are some good examples.

With three duplexes under my belt, I met my current handyman, Craig. I was perched on a roof overhang at one of my homes, priming and painting trim boards. He'd arrived at his storage shed across the alley to get some tools. We ended up talking, and soon struck up a good business relationship. Although he's not licensed or bonded, he knows quite a bit about all kinds of repair work, and his per-hour charge was *half* of what I'd found elsewhere. He does all the work that I can't or won't (as in the case of crawl spaces) do, and I trust him implicitly. Having been raised in the neighborhood, Craig was thrilled to move into one of the homes I bought seven years ago. It was a duplex, one street over from where he grew up. We converted the two-story garage into an apartment for Craig. He's very comfortable there, and when things go down in the hood, I'm glad he's nearby. For liability purposes, I had him sign a contract relieving me of responsibility if he were to get injured while on the job; I'm including a copy of it here. Check with your real estate attorney regarding a contract that will work in your jurisdiction. This is the only instance in which I've used a contract; I didn't know Craig prior to using his services. My other contractors have their own businesses and are bonded and insured. If you work with people you know, or rely on referrals, you probably won't run into contract-related problems.

INDEPENDENT CONTRACTOR AGREEMENT

This contract is being made and entered into on this _____ day of _____, _____, between Barnes Properties and _____ _____.

Said Contractor will provide certain repair, maintenance and restoration work, and assured Barnes Properties that he has the ability and resources to do such work, using tools and equipment owned by or leased to him.

He will use his own vehicle for the work.

Contractor agrees to indemnify and hold Barnes Properties and its representative harmless from any and all losses, liability, or claims by third parties (including Contractor's employees) for bodily injury, death, or property damages rising out of, during, or as a result of the services to be provided, unless caused solely by the gross negligence of Barnes Properties.

Indemnification shall include reimbursement for Barnes' attorney fees and expenses reasonably incurred in the defense of such claim.

Contactor will charge _____ for services.

If accident or emergency occurs while providing services, Contractor will contact Barnes Properties immediately. If unable to reach Barnes Properties, he shall contact _____ at _____ .

_____	_____
Barnes Properties	Independent Contractor

When acquiring a property, I make a list of work that needs to be done and estimate the cost of it before I make the offer. I don't include hourly pay to myself, but that's okay. As my learning curve goes up, I pay less and less out to others. Which means more and more money for me.

Before I get possession of a new property, I make sure that my handyman, Craig, is available every day for a week or two. His share of the job is usually done within a week. Because he does work for other people as well, I try to give him as much advance notice as possible.

Before moving to the inside of the property, I do the necessary sprucing up on the outside. I check the gutters and downspouts to make sure they're in working order, clean up any trash that's found its way into the yard, and if the weather's decent, I may do a little window and siding wash. Some of my houses have nice landscaping and some have very little. Depending on the neighborhood, you may want to invest some time and money in low-maintenance shrubbery or flowers to improve the curb-appeal of your rental property. To attract good tenants, the rental needs to look inviting from the street. If exterior paint is needed, I suggest the inexpensive store brands from Lowe's, Wal-Mart or Home Depot. They are surprisingly durable, and having checked Consumer Reports, I've found that you don't have to spend $40/gallon to get wonderful results.

Meeting some of the neighbors while doing outdoor cleanup work is a definite bonus, a great way to establish good relationships from the start. If you are adding a new roof or siding, have these contractors begin immediately.

With the house below, I considered the vinyl siding expense before putting in the offer. These are views from the back of the duplex. The siding job took two days to complete.

The first work to be done inside is always the cleanout. Many times, previous owners have left trash, broken furniture, and other assorted junk inside the house and basement, as well as out in the yard. With the help of Craig and his pickup truck, we haul the large, heavy items to the local dump. I use Costco 55-gallon heavy-duty trash bags for the smaller items. Once you've gotten the trash out, you're ready to roll.

OPERATING SYSTEMS

Before you begin the actual work on the interior of the property, you'll need to thoroughly check the furnace, electrical systems and water. You will have planned for any major heat, water or electrical expense prior to submitting your offer.

After the utilities have been turned on, have a reputable heating contractor come out to check and clean the furnace. The electrical outlets should also be checked to make sure they're getting power. There's a small tool you can buy that will indicate whether or not the outlet is "live." Of course, you can plug a small lamp or other object into each outlet and accomplish the same result.

I always check all the wall/ceiling fixtures too; where light bulbs are needed I never go above forty or sixty watts. People often use 75 watts or higher, and many fixtures aren't made to handle anything above sixty watts. If you see dark streaks above any outlet, you need to beware; that outlet probably shorted out at one time or another. GFI (ground fault interrupts) outlets should be installed in kitchens and baths, wherever there's a water source nearby. Additional kitchen outlets are often needed in older homes, to accommodate microwaves, toasters and other kitchen equipment.

Many of my rentals had older (ungrounded) outlets with only two openings for plug-ins. You can buy converters that plug into these outlets; the open end of the converter has the popular three-prong opening commonly seen in newer construction. Older outlets can easily be replaced with newer grounded outlets, too. I recommend having a licensed electrician check out everything; updates may be needed, and it's so much easier to get this done before tenants move in.

The water heater(s) should also be checked out, and the temperature set at 110 degrees; higher temperatures may cause scalding. Replacing the faucets throughout the house is a common necessity. Also, when you're having the water system checked, don't forget the outside spigot. People tend to be rough with them, and they often need to be replaced after you buy the home.

BASEMENTS AND CREEPY CRAWL SPACES

One of my 90-year-old duplexes had a basement comprised of four connected rooms. The floors were covered in a foot of rubble---dirt, trash, old papers, broken pieces of ancient furniture---and the smell emanating from the rubble was so nasty, it about knocked me over when I first looked at the house before buying it. The basement looked as if no one had been down there in forty years. I tackled this basement with my 55-gallon bags and a snow shovel. Having pinned down the source of the smell to a three-foot area, I discovered a very decayed, very dead rat under the rubble. He wasn't paying rent, so I bagged him up. If you get all the trash out and clean it well the first time, you'll have better luck at keeping your tenants from cluttering up your basement. Most basements contain the furnace, hot water heater and electrical box, and getting all the junk out will create good access to these important systems.

Many of my basements are damp and musty smelling, but hey, a basement is a basement! But if it's *wet* down there, you'll need to take care of the source of the water. Most often it's a drainage problem outside, which can be remedied by drip trays under the downspouts or adding dirt so that the ground slopes away from the foundation. If the basement's leaking like a sieve, you'll need to do what I did in the following situation.

I manage two homes near a university, for a physician in town. It's not much work on my part, and they pay me 12% of the rents as my fee. In addition to that fee, I charge them an hourly rate for any work I do at the property. They wanted to make the basement at one of the homes an extra living area, but on rainy days there were rivulets of water running down the basement walls in one area. They asked me to try and take care of it and I was able to stop the leaks with a 2-step process. UGL makes a dry powder that you mix with water and it quickly sets up like cement. It's called UGL Drylok Fast Plug™. You can actually plug an *active* leak with this stuff. They make a second product, called UGL Drylok Masonry Waterproofer™ that can be applied with a brush or roller, and it seals large areas that have been damp or wet. UGL products come in gallon-size cans, and they clean up with soap and water, which is nice. I *amazed* myself by stopping those leaks and waterproofing that basement. It currently serves as a nice extra room for the tenants, and the owner thinks I walk on water.

Crawl spaces are something I don't tackle. It's the fear of spiders thing, and I know spiders love to hang out in crawl spaces. One of my houses was built in 1863, and had a dirt floor basement and a narrow crawl. Wayne, a licensed plumber and good ol' boy from Tennessee, was taking care of a problem that Craig couldn't handle, and called me down to look at something. When I ventured down the steep wooden stairs, with the crawl on my right side, a loud hissing nearly made my heart jump into my throat. I screamed of course, and the huge opossum in the crawl space, two feet from my face, held his ground. Wayne was doubled over, beside himself with laughter. I guess the 'possum had taken up residence in the crawl, although I've no idea how he could've gotten in. Wayne informed me that they're "purty good eatin', if you "marinate 'em and bake 'em." At any rate, the 'possum may still live there today, for all I know. I'm happy to let him be.

WALLS AND CEILINGS

Before I begin the discussion on interior cosmetic fix-ups, I'd like to remind you again to tailor your fix-ups to fit in with the neighborhood. Most of the recommendations in this chapter are suitable for both low- and middle-income properties.

The first things to tackle after cleaning out the house and yard are the walls and ceilings. Occasionally, I'll come across a room with walls that are in great shape and only need to be washed. For these, I buy a product called Soilex™. I put the Soilex in one bucket and use another bucket to rinse out my wash rag. A sponge mop can be used for large areas. The nice thing about this product is it's non-sudsing and you don't have to rinse it off the wall. I start at the bottom and work up, to avoid having streaks run down from the top of the walls.

If the homes you're buying are older than fifty years, you're probably going to be dealing with large cracks here and there, from settling of the house. These are easy to repair, with drywall tape and drywall mud, or joint compound. I prefer the mesh tape to paper, because it creates a stronger repair. The mud is easily applied and smoothed out with a putty knife. On the more serious holes and cracks, a second application may be necessary, after allowing the first repair to dry overnight. This same fix can be used for ceiling cracks. If the living room or bedroom ceilings have overhead light fixtures, I highly recommend installing ceiling fans, with or without lights. Basic models don't cost much, and potential tenants are impressed when a room or two has a ceiling fan.

I'd like to interject a quick word about drop ceilings. With many older homes the ceilings are nine or ten feet high. This may look quaint, but "quaint" won't put money in your pocket. High ceilings result in higher heat bills, and they're a real hassle to paint. For these reasons, I'm always glad to see drop ceilings. The tiny apartment below used to be a basement. We fashioned a drop ceiling out of lightweight lattice, similar to what is used outdoors to conceal the area under front porches, and added a full sized egress window in the bedroom. We also closed off the HVAC and water heater, converting the basement into a cozy, comfortable one-bedroom apartment.

Several of the properties I bought had rooms with cheap, shiny paneling on the walls. Initially, I tore it off, only to find major cosmetic problems lurking behind it. If the paneling's in decent condition, buy some Kilz Primer/Stainblocker™ and just paint over it. If you use oil-base Kilz (it covers better and enables the paint to stick to the paneling better than the water-base Kilz), use a cheap, throw-away roller sleeve and handle, so you don't have to deal with trying to clean it all with mineral spirits when you're finished with the job. If you don't use primer, and just paint right over the paneling, the paint will peel off every time it gets bumped. Also, as in the case below, if the walls have been painted in bright, obnoxious colors, you may need to use Kilz on them prior to painting over them with your chosen color. If you're merely dealing with obnoxious bright paint colors on painted walls, using the water-base Kilz is fine. The hot pink and turquoise kitchen in these pictures was totally transformed by a coat of Kilz, followed by some pre-mixed Wal-Mart satin latex paint, in one of their off-white shades.

Most of my homes also had gaps around window and door trims. You can fill these with latex caulk, which is paintable and cleans up with soap and water. Don't use 100% silicone caulk; it's a bit difficult to work with, latex paint won't cover it, and mineral spirits are required to clean it up.

When you're finished with the wall and ceiling repairs, it'll be time to paint. On my first two or three homes, I used light beige for the walls, deeper beige for the window and door trim, and ceiling white for the ceilings. What was I thinking? (Another of those dumbass attacks I've talked about...) The place looked great when finished, but it took lots of time to carefully trim around the ceilings, windows and doors with the contrasting colors of paint. Rookie mistake. When a potential tenant comes to look at your apartment, do you think he cares about two-tone rooms and decorator colors? Hell no! He wants a clean place to live. I learned that I could zip through a house very quickly if I used one color for the ceiling, walls and trim. Now, the exception to this rule is if you're in a neighborhood where the comparable homes are using contrasting paint colors. Do a little snooping and find out.

If you don't have to worry about trashing nice floor coverings when you paint, I highly recommend you go with one color and use a power paint sprayer. I purchased a Wagner™ floor model that worked well. You'll need to buy a product called Floetrol™ that you add to the paint to thin it a bit, so the spray tip doesn't get clogged. Also, don't forget to cover every inch of your body and head before you start. The sprayer releases a fine spray onto the wall, but also into the room. My first spray job went well; I had a shower hat on (nice look) and my body totally covered, but my eyebrows, eyelashes and nose hairs collected an amazing amount of paint. The unit in the following photos was a perfect candidate for the power paint sprayer.

If you still like the idea of two-tone rooms, go with a very dark trim color around the windows and doors. This is very helpful when you have move-outs; the dark paint shows less dirt, greasy fingerprints, and knicks. If (and only if) I have time to spare, I use the dark trim. Also, if you're choosing single-family, middle-income homes as your target investment, you'll probably want to go with two-tone rooms, perhaps in shades of beige or taupe. As I mentioned above, look at what your competition is doing, and make sure you're equal to or one up on them. Many painters recommend applying masking tape around all the edges where the trim color meets the wall color, or the window glass. If you have a steady hand, skip the taping. I've never used it, because it takes a lot of extra time to tape edges. Just don't load your brush with too much paint when you're doing the trimming, or you'll create a mess.

What type of paint is best to use in rentals? I've found satin finish to be the best bet. Flat finish paint doesn't wipe up well. Semi-gloss cleans up well, but it also shows every defect in the wall because of its shine. You can wipe the satin finish clean, it has a very low sheen, and I recommend going with the latex variety, so that you can clean your tools and brushes with soapy water. I've found one of the best brands out there is Wal-Mart latex satin. Surprised? Well, I checked in Consumer Reports magazine a few years ago, and they rated it very high. Actually, if you check into it, you may find some of the home-improvement store brands (Lowe's,

Home Depot, etc.) are just as good. And they cost less than *half* of what the prominent brands do. I just repainted my own house with Wal-Mart and saved myself a bundle of money. They make three or four pre-mixed off-white colors. I use Country White for my rentals, which is a pleasant, creamy off-white; I stock up on it every time I go to Wal-Mart. The five-gallon buckets are too heavy for me to handle, so I stick with the one-gallon cans. The empty cans make wonderful containers for tools and other small items you need to keep with you. My trunk is filled with old paint cans being recycled this way.

I invested in a very good Werner™ four-foot ladder (anything bigger wouldn't fit well in my Corolla). It's tall enough for most painting/repair jobs in my rentals, and I'm only five feet tall. If heights are an issue with you, I'd suggest buying one of the ladders that has wide steps and a shelf on the top level for holding tools or paint. Cosco™ makes a good, heavy-duty model.

My favorite painting tools consist of a Wooster™ or Purdy™ 2 ½ inch angled brush, which is great for trimming around anything, and a Mr. Longarm International™ paint roller stick which extends 4 feet in case you're painting taller walls or ceilings. My handyman taught me to eliminate cleaning my brushes and roller sleeves by wrapping them tightly in plastic wrap if I'm going to be away from the paint job for awhile. Even if left overnight, the brush or roller sleeve won't dry out. Another timesaving tip for paint-filled brushes is to immerse them in a cup of water if you need to leave the job. Just be sure to squeeze all the water out before continuing to paint. My newest trick for saving time is to buy very cheap roller sleeves. They cost less than a dollar each, and perform as well as the more expensive types. I just throw them away when I'm done with the job instead of cleaning all the paint out of them, which takes a good while.

I don't bother with wallpaper in my rentals, because if it gets torn or marked up, it's a hassle to replace. However, a prepasted border around the ceiling adds some character to a bath or kitchen, and takes very little time to install.

To avoid having a major spill in your vehicle, make sure you replace your paint can lids tightly. Run a paintbrush along the rim to remove the excess paint, so that the lid will come off easily the next time you paint. Then, cover it with a paper towel and tap it lightly all around with a hammer, or stand on the lid to tamp it down.

You may be familiar with the health problems associated with lead base paints. If a home was built prior to 1979, chances are excellent that lead base paint was used. The good news is that simply painting over it will eliminate the problem. Very few of my homes had lead base paint on the inside, but several still had it on the exterior of the home. You can tell it by looking; the paint will be cracked vertically and horizontally, creating the look of many tiny squares all lined up next to each other. Your local board of health can cite you for lead base paint violations, so it's best to take care of the problem when you purchase the rental.

WINDOWS AND DOORS

Most older homes have older windows. They're costly to replace, and although I've done it with a couple of my rentals, I don't see replacements as a big priority in my rehabbing. Cleaning them inside and out will make them look better. Using a power washer on the outsides of them actually does a pretty good job. Caulking around the windows from the inside will help prevent air leaks in hot and cold weather. At the houses where I pay the heat bill, I used to buy the plastic window kits and cover them in the winter. Now someone has come up with clear three-inch tape that does just as well and doesn't take much time to apply. There are also products that you apply like caulk; the material is easily removed when the weather warms up. I don't worry about the warm months, because my tenants can just open the windows for a breeze. Only a few of my homes have central air; many of my tenants have never had it and don't expect it. A window air conditioner can provide a nice cool-down, and I do allow window units.

When windows get broken (and believe me, they *will* get broken from time to time) I replace them with plexi-glass, which is very sturdy and difficult to crack or break. For security purposes, do make sure all of your windows have locks that are in working order.

Screens always present a problem, because they seem to get ripped easily. Instead of trying to keep up with replacements, I supply the expandable screens where needed. On storm doors that have screens, the best thing to do is put an aluminum grill over the screened area. The grill will prevent elbows, knees, kids' toys and furniture from poking through the screen.

Some of my homes have steel core security doors, and some have solid wood doors; either style works well, but the wood door is easier to repair. I try to make sure all my entry doors have deadbolts; Qwikset™ is a good brand. If any of your doors have double-key deadbolts, replace them with the single-key type. A double-key deadbolt requires a key to be used to unlock it, from both the outside and inside. In an emergency, you don't want your tenant searching frantically for that deadbolt key.

If you're going to install storm doors, I recommend staying away from the dirt-cheap flimsy aluminum ones that are bottom-of-the-line quality. They whip and bend in the wind, get dented easily, and make the outside of your rental look crappy. For a few more dollars you can buy a heavier model that will last much longer.

Window coverings can be purchased cheaply, and they make the apartment look nicer for showings. Also, uncovered windows in a vacant house tend to invite vandals, so I prefer to shell out the cash for inexpensive curtains or mini-blinds. To save time, I buy curtains with a rod pocket that can be hung with a spring tension rod. Aluminum or vinyl mini-blinds come in a wide variety of pre-cut sizes, and can be bought inexpensively at Wal-Mart or any other large discount department store. Providing window coverings is worth it in the long run, and potential tenants appreciate the apartment being furnished with window treatments.

KITCHENS

I put major effort into making sure my kitchens and bathrooms are clean and well maintained. Whether a family is renting or buying, the woman is a driving force in the decision making, and the kitchen and bath are usually of prime importance to her. Good tenants will thoroughly check out these two rooms. In most of the homes I've purchased, stoves and refrigerators are provided, although they're not always in spiffy condition. Serious scrubbing will usually take care of the situation, unless the power's been off and food was left in the frig. When this is the case, I usually call my used appliance guy, Jimmy. He has about seven teeth, sports a five-star mullet and smells a little funky on hot summer days, but his products are clean and he'll remove the old appliance for me, too. For stoves, the Easy Off™ stove and oven cleaner products work well. Just be sure to buy the fume-free kind. The original scent makes me wheeze like a four-pack-a-day smoker. Most of my kitchens don't have range hoods; you can always install a hood vent, but they don't seem to be very effective. I don't bother installing a vent. The wall above the stovetop does get grease spots, but I just clean the wall and paint it when someone moves out. The other alternative is to purchase aluminum (or other) adhesive or decorative tiles and apply them to the wall above the stove.

I'd like to address the new/used appliance issue for a moment. New appliances are costly, and most cities have used appliance stores. I highly recommend you find a source for the used variety. You can check the yellow pages, or pick up one of those free local newspapers and find a supplier. If you have a storage garage (I use a garage at one of my properties for this purpose) you can pick up bargains here and there, and store them until needed. I always supply the stove and refrigerator at my lower-end properties; many potential tenants don't have appliances of their own. If the refrigerator comes with an icemaker, take it out. Why mess with hooking up the water line, when there's a good chance the icemaker will malfunction after awhile? Try to minimize your repair issues. This also applies to stoves. Avoid the bells and whistles, and keep it simple when you can.

If your market segment is likely to have their own appliances, then by all means forego the expense of supplying them. I don't provide washers or dryers, and actually, many of my apartments don't have hookups. If a good tenant wants the convenience of washer/dryer hookups, I get a quote on the work and have the tenant split the cost with me. Having the washer and dryer hookup does increase the value of the apartment, and higher rent can be charged.

Some of my homes have old porcelain kitchen sinks, which I don't replace unless they're an eyesore. They're sturdy and they clean up well, and you can buy touch-up paint for chips in the porcelain. If a new sink is necessary, I prefer the stainless steel variety. They're durable and easy to clean. I've stopped equipping them with hand-held sprayer attachments; they don't hold up well, and I've gotten tired of fixing and replacing them. Garbage disposals are a nice amenity, but I don't put them in, because they're often troublesome down the road, when some little kid stuffs them with toys or bubble gum. Keep it simple.

Initially, Craig installed cheap, plastic faucets in kitchens and baths.

Totally not worth it. They leak after a while because they're not well made, the plastic cracks and peels, and it's much smarter to furnish all your sinks with basic stainless steel faucets, such as the Delta™ lower-end models.

Most of my kitchens come with painted wood cabinets. A few still have the old metal cabinets, too. Before you tear everything out, consider what a creative paint job might do to revitalize the look of your kitchen. It's amazing what a little paint and funky new hardware can do to spruce up old cabinets and make the kitchen the focal point of the entire house. The insides of the cabinets may be grungy, but if you clean them out, paint them, and apply Magic Cover™ shelf liner, they look great. Magic Cover is self-adhesive, but can be repositioned easily and doesn't drive me crazy by sticking to *itself* better anything else. Contact paper makes me want to scream.

If you need new cabinetry, I recommend inexpensive, simple wood that can be painted. If you prefer stained wood, you can find decent ones that are inexpensive. Formica™ and other more contemporary types are more money, and your tenants will be happy with something basic, as long as it's clean and looks nice.

To enhance the inexpensive wood cabinets below, you might add two-tone paint and/or interesting hardware.

If you choose higher-end rental property as your investment choice, you'll need to provide more upgrades. Central air, dishwashers, garbage disposals, ceramic tile, etc. may be present in other homes in the area, and you need to be competitive in order to attract tenants. Shop around for closeout deals and other bargains, and when determining rent prices, charge what the traffic will bear. Be aware, however, that pouring more upgrades into the property doesn't guarantee higher rents.

A word to the wise….when cleaning dirty appliances, sinks, toilets, etc. buy a good pair of rubber gloves and *use them*. There's no telling how many nasty little germs are lurking in the scum. The thin latex ones like they use in hospitals are the most comfortable. As far as cleaning products, I do have a few favorites. Krud Kutter™ does exactly what its name implies…it cuts the crud. The spray bottle is easy to use, and I buy this product in gallon containers and just refill the spray bottle. Krud Kutter will break up all kinds of dirt and grease throughout the house, whether it's on countertops, toilets, floors or walls. I even use it at my own home on clothing and carpet stains. Barkeepers Friend™ works best for scouring the insides of toilets and sinks. It comes in a shaker-type can, and I like it better than the other name brands. These products may be found at home improvement stores, hardware stores and department stores like Wal-Mart, Target and Meijer.

When I'm faced with sticky situations like syrup that has run down the frig walls and settled in the bottom, or unknown sticky stuff on walls or floors, my five-in-one tool works well in conjunction with the Krud Kutter. A few years back, after evicting some filthy tenants, I noticed some heavy syrupy stuff that had run down the insides of their frig. When I pulled out the vegetable drawer at the bottom of the appliance, I found about two hundred dead cockroaches, belly up. At least they enjoyed their last meal. My five-in-one tool scraped them up nicely, and Krud Kutter took care of the rest of the mess. The five-in-one tool (now they have eight- and ten-in-one tools, too) has a flat, beveled edge that serves as a great scraper; it also performs a variety of other tasks. Buy one at any home improvement store and explore the opportunities.

BATHROOMS

The bathroom holds a lot of cleaning challenges. Tubs that haven't been scrubbed in months, toilets with layers of crust and splatters, urine-stained vinyl floors… you name it, I've dealt with it. Squatters had inhabited the upstairs apartment of a vacant, neglected foreclosure I bought. Although there was no heat, electricity or water, people had gotten in somehow. There was trash and drug paraphernalia scattered everywhere. When I lifted the toilet seat, it was obvious they'd been using it and throwing dirt over the excrement. It was totally filled, to the rim. Craig's and my first task was to unbolt it, carry it out and get rid of it. We struggled to carry it down the stairs. I had the bowl end, and worked hard at breathing through my mouth. When Craig went back up to check the wax ring etc. in the floor, he realized the way it was set, we were going to have to use *that* toilet. You can imagine my dismay. I took care of it, but am thankful I don't have a weak stomach. Toilets are cheap. If you're confronted with a super nasty situation, replace the toilet if you can. The newer, low-flow models are most economical.

All toilets and sinks in the home should be equipped with shut-off valves. In an emergency situation, it's always helpful to be able to shut off the water at the source of the problem.

Some of my units have really old bathtubs. It's way too costly to have them replaced, but for a few hundred dollars you can have them resurfaced, and I've done this with several of mine. Replacing the tub surround also gives the tub area a nice face-lift, and decent tub surround kits can be bought for under $100. Many newer homes will be equipped with one-piece fiberglass showers and tubs. If they're in terrible shape, they can also be resurfaced, but if they're just filthy and grimy, Easy Off oven cleaner cuts right through the grime, soap scum and hard water stains. It works. Spray it on, leave it for a few hours, and scrub it off later. For porcelain tubs and toilets, I've heard pool chlorine works well, if you pour it in and, again, let it sit. Initially, I thought I'd have to resurface the bathtub below. Easy Off took care of it!

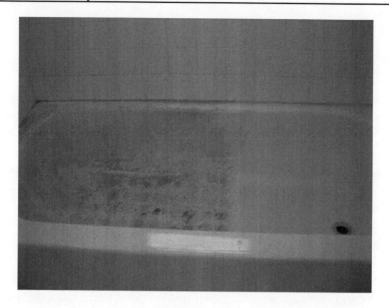

Another product that is surprisingly effective on fiberglass and porcelain surfaces is toilet bowl cleaner. One of my contractors shared this tip with me. The next time I was faced with a nasty fiberglass shower, I bought Extra Strength SnoBowl™ and poured some of it on the floor of the shower. I left the area to get a scrub brush, and by the time I got back, the floor beneath the SnoBowl was clean! What a great surprise. I hadn't even scrubbed it.

Some of the older homes have no showerheads at all. In the olden days, people just took baths. In these situations, you can buy a shower attachment kit. If the walls aren't conducive to having a shower curtain, you can buy a stainless steel oval ring that can be suspended from the ceiling; the curtain, which I always supply, can be hung from it.

Some of my units have the original porcelain bath sinks, but I've replaced most of them with inexpensive sinks and base cabinets. These can be bought together in one big box, in a variety of sizes. Buy a Delta™ or other basic stainless steel bath faucet to go with it. When I rent to smokers, they'll sometimes rest a cigarette on the edge of the sink and forget about it, creating a brown stain on the sink. No amount of scrubbing with Barkeepers Friend will remove that stain, but I found something else that will. Buy some heavy-duty plumbers' screen (ask for it at the hardware store) and use it like sandpaper on the stain; it will fade out. Many of my bathrooms don't have exhaust fans, but if there's a window in the room I don't install one.

FLOORS

The last thing on the long list of repairs is the floor. When your flooring is done, your apartment should be ready for tenants. I don't use ceramic tile, due to the expense involved in buying and installing it. I prefer carpet to hardwood floors, so when I buy a house with wood floors, I don't bother getting them refinished. Wood floors are much noisier than carpet, and with multiple apartments in one house, I try to cut down on noise as much as possible. If single-family rentals are your niche and hardwoods/ceramic tile are prevalent in your neighborhood, you'll need to explore those possibilities in order to be competitive.

I've experimented quite a bit with different flooring options, and have come up with the most durable and economic solutions. For all rooms except the kitchen and bathroom, a Berber or level loop carpet will last the longest. Shags and plush carpets show wear much quicker, with a lot of matting down in traffic areas. If your apartment has stairs going up to a second floor, by all means carpet them. This cuts down on noise and looks much better than bare wood. *Never* go with light colors. I prefer something dark, maybe with a small pattern. Sticking with something close to the color of dirt, like dark brown or gray, is a brilliant choice. To keep my tenants from tracking in, I always put a mat just inside the door. My friends give me their slightly used mats and throw rugs to use in my apartments. They're practical, and potential tenants feel the rugs make the rental look homey. It's also a good idea to have a vinyl or tile entry area installed at the front and back doors. The scrubbable entry and a doormat will save wear and tear on your carpets. As I mentioned above, you need to be competitive with other rentals in your area...flooring is an important part of an applicant's first impression of your rental. Make choices that are not only durable and affordable, but attractive as well.

You can get years out of your carpet if you follow the above suggestions. My carpet installer works full time but does side work. His price is reasonable, and he can often pick up bargains and closeouts for me through his store. Sometimes he gets mill returns from his store, and they are willing to get rid of them for $2 or $3/yard. Even if the color is a little lighter than I'd like, I jump on this deal. The quality is usually very good, so it's totally worth it for that kind of money. Also, many carpet stores sell remnants. My carpet supplier buys my favorite in super-large rolls, and charges me less than he does the general public. This is an example of how telling contractors you have several properties can work for your benefit.

Purchasing your own carpet shampooer will save you lots of money. Bissell™ made my first model, followed by a Eureka™, and currently I have one made by Hoover™. All are good brands and were under $200; the key is to find a shampooer that's portable. Most of the ones I've seen are just way too heavy to carry and maneuver into and out of the back of my car. Because everything in today's world seems to be made of plastic (which does create portability) my shampooers don't last more than a few years. But when I think of the hundreds of dollars I'd spend having a company do the carpet cleaning every time, it's no big deal to buy a new machine every few years.

For kitchens, I recommend staying away from sheet vinyl, unless you use a high-quality, heavy-duty type of vinyl. Carelessness with cigarettes can create burn marks, tenants move things across it and rip holes in it, and then you're faced with replacing the whole room. I've had a little better success with sheet vinyl in bathrooms, but I wouldn't recommend it. I don't use ceramic tile because I haven't found a cheap way to buy it or have it installed. For now, I prefer commercial tile. It's very durable, can withstand a lot of abuse, and it's easy to clean. I've also used the peel-and-stick variety, and this type of flooring holds up pretty well. If the floor's fairly level, the peel-and-stick tiles are simple to install yourself. The beauty of the peel-and-stick tiles is that if one or two get damaged, you can replace them easily. I tiled many kitchens and baths with these early on, and have started having the commercial type put in because of its long-term durability. When someone moves out and the floor (vinyl or tile) is dirty, the good old-fashioned string mop does a better job than any other kind of mop on the market. Spraying Krud Kutter on the floor and damp mopping usually takes care of it. I do everything I can to avoid the on-your-hands-and-knees scrub job.

LOCKS AND KEYS

After I'd accumulated a few rental properties, the key-juggling issue was clearly becoming a problem. So I converted my rentals to a master key system. I have one master key that unlocks the front door of all my apartments. I don't spend the extra money to master the back doors. When I get my doors rekeyed, the locksmith makes a tenant key (which is different than the master key) that will unlock every door into the apartment. I make sure I get a copy of that tenant key for myself, too. The tenant keys are all tagged and kept in a box in my trunk. As a safety measure, I write the house number on the tag, but not the street name. In the event someone broke into my car, they wouldn't have complete addresses to my homes. The only key I need on a daily basis is my master key. My trusted repair people also have a copy of the master key, which saves me time and gas money. When repairs are needed, all I do is call them, and they'll take care of the repair and send me a bill. This is particularly helpful when I'm out of town. (Yes, I do take vacations! More about that later...). Whether you're home or away, make sure you have a complete list of your repair peoples' names and contact numbers with you at all times.

Some property owners choose to install lock boxes at their properties. They keep a copy of the apartment key inside, and when a repairperson needs to gain access to the apartment, the owner gives him/her the keypad code that will open the box. Potential tenants could even view the apartment this way, but I'd prefer to meet in person.

So at this point, you're just about ready to start landlording. If you've been willing to do a majority of the work yourself, you've already made and saved yourself a boatload of money. I can't emphasize the importance of this enough...getting an excellent return on your investment requires hard work and sacrifice. Paying someone else to do what you can do yourself makes no sense. If you want to maximize your return, do what you can on your own.

I work on one side of a duplex at a time, so that I can get at least one apartment up and running. It's nice to make some rental income while I work on completing the other apartment(s) in the property. When you're close to finishing the first unit, it's time to begin looking for that fortunate soul who gets to be your tenant.

THE BOTTOM LINE

You'll feel overwhelmed as you tackle your first rehabbing job, but if you break it down into small segments like I've done in this chapter, it'll feel more manageable. After you've done a couple of units, whether they're single- or multi-family properties, the fix-up process will become routine.

As you move through the fix-up, be aware of what the surrounding rentals look like inside. If there are others for rent in the area, check out the competition by looking in the windows, attending their open houses, or setting up appointments to see them. When you're rehabbing, it's important that you measure up to your competition. If you don't, your rental will stand empty.

I'd suggest you take before and after photos. This part of the job is both challenging and rewarding, and you'll be pleased and amazed by the transformation that takes place as you move through the rehab process.

CHAPTER SEVEN
THE FINE ART OF FINDING GOOD TENANTS

THE YOUNG WOMAN HAD parked her 15-year-old rusted-out Ford Pinto two doors down from my rental. She got out, trailing three grimy, barefoot toddlers behind her. Peeking out the window of my rental property, I hoped she was visiting someone next door. Alas, she was coming to apply for my apartment. I kindly showed it to her. The filthy feet and grubby little hands and faces of her kids indicated what my walls and floors would look like if they rented that apartment. I passed on that applicant.

For the purpose of this chapter, I'm assuming you've decided to manage your own properties, at least for now. Doing it yourself will save money and ensure that your business is being run in the appropriate manner. Down the road, if you 1) don't have the time, or 2) don't have the desire, then hiring a property manager will lighten the load. I'll address that issue later.

ADVERTISING

As I mentioned earlier in this guide, a significant number (40%) of Americans earn under $35,000/year. Because they may be be renters throughout their lives, a nice, clean apartment accompanied by an attentive landlord is a wonderful find. Landlords often get a bad rap and I have to admit, there *are* some true slumlords out there, in every city. They give the rest of us a bad name. I respect all people who work hard and try to create a good life for themselves and their families, and this is reflected in the way I treat my tenants. I love my work, and enjoy being able to provide people with quality apartments.

The challenge is finding great tenants who will take care of the apartment and pay rent in a timely manner. So, how can you assist these great tenants in finding you? Here's what has worked for me.

1) **Put a sign in the yard.** You may have one made at a sign shop, or buy your own For Rent sign at your local home improvement store, and include your phone and number of bedrooms in the blank space provided on the sign. You might try the open house idea and see what it brings. With my first rental, I tried advertising an open house on Sunday afternoon as a way to draw tenants. For the most part, it was a waste of my time. I got very few serious applicants from the open house. It's also helpful to print out an information sheet about the apartment. You can buy a plastic tube or box for the sheets, which will clip on to the side of the sign. Here's a sample of what you might include on the info sheet:

41 NORTH ADDISON, DUPLEX

2 bedrooms
1 full bath with tub and shower
Stove and refrigerator
Washer/dryer hookups
New carpet
Fresh paint
Newer gas furnace
Eat-in kitchen
½ basement
Garage
No pets

$500/month plus heat and electricity
We pay water/sewer
$300 deposit up front

Available July 1
Call Barb at xxx-xxxx for more information

2) **Put an ad in the paper.** Many of my tenants don't subscribe to the daily or Sunday newspaper and the ad cost is high, so I avoid advertising there. My best route has been to advertise in the local free newspaper that comes out once a week. Most towns have a free paper, which is usually distributed to gas stations and grocery stores in the area. I get lots of calls this way, and there's a nominal fee for the ad. A sample of what I include would be: "1525 Wilcox, large two bedroom ½ double, stove and frig, washer/dryer hookups, $250 bi-weekly plus heat and electric, $300 deposit up front, no pets, excellent condition, xxx-xxx-xxxx." Make sure you can be reached at the number you include in your ad. If your ad includes your home number and you have a cell phone, your outgoing message on your home phone should give the cell number as an alternative if you're not home. When a potential tenant calls and can't reach you, he'll move on to the next ad on his list, and you may have lost a wonderful tenant.

3) **Networking.** This is a *great* way to find good tenants. When I have an empty apartment coming up, I write a note to all my top tenants (clean people who pay on time) and tell them the particulars of the apartment. Often, they have friends who may be looking for a place to rent, and I trust they won't steer me wrong. I've found many new tenants this way, which is preferable to taking a chance with a total stranger. Some landlords give a cash reward if their tenant brings them another good tenant. I've not gone that route because I can get the same result without any money leaving my greedy little hands! Networking through neighborhood establishments is also an effective option. Community centers, churches, small shops or food stores often have bulletin boards where local people can post a variety of for sale or for rent signs. If your rental is near a large business establishment, try to post a flier on the premises. People love having the option of being able to walk to work. When a potential tenant calls you, *always* ask where they heard about the apartment. This will show you what type of advertising is working best for you.

DISCRIMINATE

Or, maybe I should rephrase that. *Be discriminating!* When someone comes to one of your apartments and likes what they see, take a good look at *them* and decide whether *you* like what *you* see. Do they appear to have washed their hair and brushed their teeth in the past twenty-four hours? Are their clothes clean? Do they have three weeks' worth of grime under their fingernails? Do they smell like stale (or fresh) alcohol? Marijuana? Are they surly and argumentative? Did they drive to your apartment? If so, what does that car look like? Is it dirty inside and out? Is it held together with duct tape? Is there a vast array of trash, fast food wrappers, etc. strewn about the interior? If so, you can assume they'll treat your apartment the same way. If children are present, are they wild and unruly? Have they taken a bath recently? In the case of potential tenants, you often *can* judge a book by its cover.

The above-mentioned factors may negatively affect your business relationship with your tenant, so feel free to *not* consider people who'll have a hard time holding up their end of the lease agreement. Aside from their looks (I'm talking about cleanliness only) and attitudes, there are other areas where discrimination is legal:

1) **Ability to pay.** If they bring home $800/month and the rent is $600, the math just isn't going to work out for them. Other expenses will eat up the remaining $200 in the blink of an eye. My potential tenant's gross pay must be at least two and a half times the rent. If not, it may be difficult to make ends meet, especially if they have other debt. Car payments, child support and garnishments of wages are common debts owed, and you must take them into consideration. Sometimes tenants aren't realistic about their ability to pay, so you need to be realistic for them. Credit reports may be obtained through websites. If your target tenant is a middle income person, you may find credit reports worthwhile. Many people have bad credit or no credit, and I don't pursue credit checks. I've rented to some wonderful people who had no credit; don't rule someone out for having no credit. Paying cash and living without credit cards is not a bad thing! If a potential tenant has bad credit problems, listen to the story, verify what you can, then go with your gut.

2) **Number and type of vehicles**. You can limit the number of vehicles permitted on your property. You can also deny renting to someone who has a very noisy vehicle. For example, you have to allow motorcycles, but you don't have to allow noisy motorcycles.

3) **Past tenant record**. As you'll see on my application, I request the current landlord's phone number. Listen closely to what the landlord says, if he/she seems to be a reputable person. I usually ask if the tenant has been paying on time, and whether the apartment has been well maintained by the tenant. You may deny tenancy if your applicant has been late with payments or the apartment was poorly maintained. You may decide to require past tenancies of at least six months or a year if you wish; this is your right.

4) **Honesty/attitude**. If the person has lied to you about anything on the application, he/she can be denied tenancy. I've had people write their friends' names and numbers in the work supervisor section of the application. When I call the business number and the person answers with an unprofessional "Yeah?" I know they're masquerading as the supervisor. When someone tells you they've been at their current job for a year and your call to their boss determines they've just completed their second week, feel free to toss their application. Attitude includes many of the things mentioned above, including cleanliness. Like the woman in my story above, if the applicant is filthy, you may decide they don't meet your cleanliness requirement. (I've never had to turn someone down specifically for this reason; there's always another applicant who's financially more capable, thank goodness.)

5) **Number of tenants**. You may limit the number of people to occupy your apartment. For instance, four is my maximum number for a two-bedroom place. You can't deny renting to someone because they have kids, but you can deny renting a two-bedroom apartment to someone with a *slew* of kids. It's amazing how unrealistic people can be about this issue. I've had applicants inquire about a two-bedroom apartment, and when I ask them, "For how many people?" they reply, "Six." I tell them I'm sorry, but we can't put more than four people in a two-bedroom apartment.

6) **Personal habits**. Although I rent to smokers, you may choose not to and be within your legal rights. You may even refuse to rent to people who drink more than two or three drinks/day if you choose. (I don't know how you'd monitor this one...the honor system?) Needles to say, illegal drugs are never welcome.

7) **Job history**. This is another area where discrimination is welcome. Some landlords require at least a year with the same source of income, but I'm more lenient. I require at least six months at the same job, but have made exceptions occasionally, if someone had a long-term job and recently switched, for a valid reason.

Discrimination and prejudice have a definite place in your framework for finding tenants. The above points are valid, and if you're discriminating in these areas, you'll save yourself a ton of headaches later on. But be aware of the many areas in which you can *not* discriminate:

1) **Race**
2) **Religion**
3) **Sex**
4) **Age**
5) **Nationality**
6) **Physical disability**

I welcome all applicants without regard to the above list. A very pleasant woman called me one day to inquire about one of my rentals. She asked several questions and had a friend in the background that prompted her with additional questions from time to time. She seemed like a great candidate. As we wrapped up the conversation, she shocked me with the following.

"So, do you rent to black people?"

After I recovered from the shock, I replied, tongue-in-cheek, "No, I'm sorry....I only rent to people who are green or purple."

There was dead silence, then raucous laughter from all three of us. Then I proceeded to tell her she should never feel the need to ask that question of anyone, and that it's her right to live anywhere she pleases. We met at the apartment the following day. Another word about race and discrimination…when an applicant asks you about your rental neighborhood in regard to racial mix, don't comment. This is racial profiling and discrimination. I give directions to the house and tell them they're welcome to drive by. This is good advice to all of your applicants. They may call you back if they'd like to look inside and meet you to fill out an application. If your neighborhood and rentals are safe and well maintained, you'll be able to attract good tenants.

The U.S. Department of Housing and Urban Development (HUD) puts out a free newsletter describing recent updates in fair housing. HUD can be reached at 1-800-343-3442.

In addition to these federal anti-discrimination laws, some states bar discrimination regarding sexual orientation, marital status, occupation, politics, etc. To find out more, contact your local department of fair employment and housing.

THE APPLICATION (KEEP IT SIMPLE)

Before I share my application with you, let me tell you about some of the situations I've encountered with my tenants. People are often shocked when they learn I don't run credit checks on potential tenants. Investor friends with higher-income properties use agencies such as Experian (www.experian.com; 888-397-3742) to find out about credit histories. As I mentioned above, I find credit checks to be a waste of my time because some of my applicants have shaky credit, or no credit. Some of them have never had a checking account or savings account. While I initially found this amazing, I've learned it's not necessarily a bad thing. Paying cash for items instead of paying with plastic isn't a bad thing.

A few of my tenants have had money problems and even bankruptcy in the past. Many of them don't own credit cards and some have had run-ins with the law. In other words, a few of my renters have had bad luck or have made poor decisions in the past. (Haven't we all?) If you wait for a renter with perfect credit and a totally untarnished past, you'll die waiting. My main concern is about the *recent* past. What's their current living situation? Have they been good renters? Are they stable in their jobs, and have they held them for at least six months to a year? I understand that for some renters, living from paycheck to paycheck is the best they can do. This is why I allow them to pay rent weekly if they get paid weekly. (I'll discuss rents in the next chapter.) I'm more than willing to provide them with a nice, clean apartment, if I'm impressed with what I learn from checking out the information they give me on their application.

Landlording by Leigh Robinson contains several forms that are useful in the landlording business. I've tweaked and retweaked my forms through the years and am delighted with the results. Feel free to use and tweak mine, as well. *Sharing all forms with a good real estate attorney is a wise move; he/she may suggest changes that reflect local statutes.* Here's a copy of my application.

APPLICATION

Rental Application for _____ (address)

Name_____ Date of Birth _____

SS#_____Drivers Lic. # _____

Marital Status_____Current Address _____

Landlord Name & Phone_____

Rental Amount_____Reason for Moving_____

Where do you work?_____How long?_____

Supervisor's name & phone _____

How much income do you TAKE HOME per week/bi-weekly/ monthly?_____

If person to share apt. has a job:

Name_____ Date of Birth _____

SS#_____Drivers Lic. # _____

Where employed?_____How long?_____

Supervisor's name & phone _____

How much income do you TAKE HOME per week/bi-weekly/ monthly?_____

NO PETS ALLOWED

List every person (name and age) who will live with you:

_____

When would you like to move in? _____

Personal References (Name, address & Phone)

_____

_____

_____

Child Support: How much do you pay?_____Receive? _____

Garnishments taken out of your pay?_____ How much? _____

Accounts owed: (car, furniture, loans, etc,)

_____Amt. Per Month_____

_____Amt. Per Month_____

Do you have any accounts with a bank?

Type of Account_____Name of bank_____

I certify that the above information is true, and I authorize a credit and reference check.

Signature_____ Date _____

As you proceed to check out the application, you'll find the key elements are the rental and work references, and the big bottom line... do they have enough income to rent your apartment? Has the person been dependable at work? Punctual? If the employer is a large firm, you may be referred to Human Resources to verify the applicant's work history. Human Resources will tell you the start date and wage earned, but nothing else. If possible, I talk to the person's immediate supervisor, who is often willing to give honest comments about the applicant. (Work ethic, punctuality, etc.) I like having the applicant furnish a paycheck stub when he fills out the application. This will show his take-home pay, which is very important. The current landlord is the other valuable reference on the application. Has your applicant paid rent on time? If he's gotten behind, has he caught it up quickly? Does he keep his apartment clean? Is he quiet enough that neighbors aren't bothered? Positive responses to these questions are essential if I'm going to take the person on as a tenant. Another thing I do is drive by the place they're currently renting. If it's a run-down dump, the tenant doesn't care much about his surroundings, does he? That's a definite red flag. The personal references section serves me well if someone leaves my apartment later on without paying, and has left some junk or other items inside the apartment. I contact the references in an effort to track down the tenant.

If the potential tenants are boyfriend/girlfriend and they both have jobs, I try to make sure that at least one of them makes enough income to allow him/her to stay if the relationship would fall apart. Ideally, that person should sign the lease. I ask how long they've been together and try to get a feel for the depth of the relationship, but there's no guarantee the couple will stay a couple.

Beware of the person who calls about the apartment and says, "I have the money right now. Can I meet you there and sign a lease today?" If they're willing to rent a place sight unseen, they're desperate. Are they being evicted from another apartment? You don't need them as tenants.

When someone wants to see one of my apartments and we agree to meet there the following day at 4 o'clock, I tell them to touch base with me sometime around noon to verify their arrival at the designated time. I've wasted way too much time and gasoline on no-shows. I try to show the apartment to as many prospective tenants as possible, on the same day at the same time. Because of work schedules, people are more available on the weekend.

When one of your places is sitting empty, it's tempting to rent it to someone, anyone. You're not making money, and this frustration may drive you to rent to a poor candidate. Don't do it! You'll be sorry. If you have poor candidates hounding you, you may tell them they don't fit the tenant guidelines you've established. Or, put them off by telling them you're processing the applications and it's going to take a while to get through them. Or you might tell them you're holding the apartment for a former tenant who is planning on moving back to town. Don't lie and tell them the apartment's been rented if it hasn't.

I've had to turn down hundreds of applicants through the years, for a variety of reasons. Most of the time, it's because they don't make enough money to rent my apartment, or they haven't been at their current job long enough. Other times, it may be a cleanliness, honesty or attitude issue. All of these are deal breakers.

I'd like to add a word about personal safety here. I'm sometimes too trusting of people and situations, and this can lead to problems. I refused to carry a gun for protection, so friends bought me pepper spray, which was always buried somewhere in the glove compartment of my car. (A lot of good it'll do me *there*.) Whether you're male or female, if you're working alone, be aware of your surroundings, and when you're renovating or redoing an apartment, keep the door locked. When showing an apartment, have the applicant walk in ahead of you rather than behind. A few years ago, I was threatened by one of my tenants who was being evicted. He verbally threatened me over the phone, and even enlisted his elderly father's help with the phone threats. Although this has happened only once in my career, I decided to remove my home address from the phone book. The only address my tenants have is my post office box. You may never be faced with a threatening situation, but taking your personal safety for granted is a mistake, regardless of where you are.

Many times, people will ask, "Will you work with me on the deposit? I can give you $100 now, and the rest next week." Well, next week never comes. I learned the hard way, after trusting I'd get the entire deposit when promised. The idea behind the deposit is that, if stuff hits the fan and you end up evicting the tenant, at least you'll keep the deposit to help pay back rent owed to you. So get the entire amount up front. The eviction process in my area takes about two and a half weeks, so I usually charge at least two and a half weeks' rent as the deposit amount. We'll discuss evictions later.

DON'T SHOOT THE MESSENGER

Building good relationships is essential to running a successful business. You'll get much more out of your tenants if they 1) like you and 2) respect you. The tough part is establishing and maintaining enough emotional distance between you and the tenant. I'm an extrovert, and I choose to think the best in people and in situations. Early on in my career I allowed myself to get overly involved in the lives of some tenants. This mistake caused me to make decisions on an emotional rather than practical basis, which cost me dearly in the end. We're talking thousands of dollars in lost rents over the first few years of my career. When tenants were facing hardships and got behind on rent payments, I often let them slide, believing their promise to catch up the next week. As I mentioned above, next week never comes. Not often enough, anyway. Another week goes by, another $100 down the toilet. Another week passes, another flush. My sympathetic attitude prevailed over good business sense, and I allowed myself to get too close to some of the tenants. Maybe social work was my true calling. Anyway, I've learned there's a fine line I mustn't cross. Be friendly. Be fair. But don't be a friend.

Even if you've established good emotional boundaries with your tenants, you'll face a plethora of other issues as the landlord. Some tenants will push the limits of the lease, and push the limits of the landlord. One of my most brilliant business practices is this: *Don't let your tenants know you're the owner of the property*. When your tenant is angry about something concerning his tenancy, it's nice to have him believe you're merely the property manager, not the person who makes all the decisions. (Don't shoot the messenger.) The final decisions are up to the owner. This little ploy has worked wonders for me through the years. It takes the heat off me in a variety of situations:

- My tenant has begged me to let her have a cat. I listen sympathetically, and though we have a no pets clause in our lease, I agree to talk to the owner about it and see if he's willing to relent, since she's been a terrific tenant.

- My tenant has gotten behind in his rent, for the second time. It took longer than promised to catch it up the first time, and I'm just not willing to put up with it again. (Show me the money!) He begs and promises. I listen sympathetically, and agree to go to bat for him with the owner.

- My forty-five year old hippie tenant has his Grateful Dead music playing so loud it's rattling the windows of the apartment. The neighbors have complained once before and I threatened eviction if it would happen again. He directs his anger and frustration at me, and I feel uneasy in his presence. Although I have every intention of filing eviction on him, he calms down when I tell him I'll talk with the owner about giving him one more chance. (Don't hold your breath on that one, buddy.)

I truly enjoy my work and my tenants, and it's helpful for them to feel we're in this together. They know I work hard, and the camaraderie that exists between us is a wonderful thing. The tenants see me as their ally in many situations; if they knew I'm the owner, the dynamics of our relationship might change dramatically. They might pre-judge me as the wealthy, disinterested owner instead of the compassionate go-between who cares about them and their apartment.

I once had a tenant who complained constantly. Her apartment was always a mess, she found things to whine about on a daily basis, was very demanding, never on time with her rent (this was before I cracked down on delinquent payers) and she was slowly driving me crazy. She demanded to speak with the owner at one point and I told her he lived out of state. Surely she wouldn't want to talk to him badly enough to make a long distance call. She insisted, so I gave her my brother-in-law John's phone number. I hung up and immediately called John, told him the story and how to respond. Now, John's a no-nonsense guy who doesn't put up with much from anyone. I instructed him to be kind but firm, and he agreed. John did a great job until the tenant started screaming at him, and then he let her have it, threatening to have me file eviction the next day. Interestingly enough, the tenant never gave me any trouble after that! But I did evict her for non-payment. If you decide to keep your ownership of the property a private matter, I suggest you have someone in mind who's willing to act as owner if someone asks for his number.

Another benefit of being just the property manager is that it buys me time when people have requests I need to think about instead of responding immediately. Being somewhat softhearted, I've agreed to things in the moment and then regretted doing so later, after taking time to think through all the pros and cons. Saying "Let me talk to the owner about it and I'll get back to you in a couple days" buys me the time I need to make good decisions. And sometimes I do bend the rules when I'm dealing with a wonderful tenant whom I trust.

I should mention here that most of the horror stories detailed in this book occurred during the early years of my career, when I suffered an incredibly large number of dumbass attacks. Hopefully, the lessons contained in this guide will prevent you from having your own share of these attacks.

THE BOTTOM LINE

Once your rental property is in superb condition, it's time to search for the superb tenant. Be thorough in your advertising efforts; networking with your other good tenants is always an effective approach, along with yard signs, newspaper ads and postings in local stores, businesses, churches, etc.

The majority of my tenants over the years have been wonderful, hardworking people. It's the frustrating minority that can wear you down and cause burnout, which I'll discuss in the next chapter. Finding that perfect tenant isn't an exact science, but if you use a good application, some common sense, and a little bit of going with your gut, you'll end up with decent tenants more often than not.

CHAPTER EIGHT

FAST FOOD LIVING
(GETTING 'EM IN, GETTING 'EM OUT)

PEOPLE GET BURNED OUT in this business. Most of the time, it's due to tenant issues. Tenant issues arise because key points haven't been addressed in the lease, or because the landlord isn't willing to enforce the lease. A few short months of ineffective tenant management can leave you feeling exhausted, crazed, and totally burned out. If you have a great, airtight lease like mine, and if you're willing to enforce it, the "b" word won't be in your vocabulary.

When you make arrangements to meet your new tenant at the apartment, you'll bring:

1) two copies of the lease
2) two tenant keys (keep a third for yourself)
3) required local/federal disclosure forms
4) receipt book

Another item you may want to include is a written inspection checklist, camera, or video recorder to document the condition of the apartment upon move-in. If you're using a video recorder, make sure your tenant is included in the recording. Before you go through the lease with your tenant, conduct a walk-through and complete this part of the process. When my tenant moves out, they may forget that the fist-size hole in the bedroom drywall wasn't there when they moved in. My written inspection form (which they've signed) will help them remember. I'm including a simple inspection list here.

INSPECTION FORM

LIVING ROOM

____Carpet/flooring, window coverings, walls, ceiling, lights in good shape and clean.
Concerns _____

KITCHEN

____Flooring, window coverings, walls, ceiling, lights, appliances, sink & counter in good shape and clean.
Concerns _____

BATHROOM

____Flooring, window coverings, walls, ceiling, lights, tub and sink in good shape and clean.
Concerns _____

BEDROOM

____Carpet, walls, ceiling, closet, window coverings, lights in good shape and clean.
Concerns _____

BEDROOM

____Carpet, walls, ceiling, closet, window coverings, lights in good shape and clean.
Concerns _____

OTHER POSSIBLE ISSUES

_____

_____   _____
Tenant Signature   Date

THE AIRTIGHT LEASE

WARNING: If you think you can get by with a lease purchased at an office supply store or plucked out of a book, think again! Before you come up with your own airtight lease, network with your local landlord association and real estate attorney to find out what forms are commonly used in your area. Landlord/tenant ordinances vary from state to state and county to county, and it's important that you be in compliance with both state and local statutes. That being said, many of the components in my lease will be suitable throughout the country.

Before I rented out my first apartment, I combed through several books on real estate management, searching for the lease that would suit my needs as a landlord. Basically, I wanted the authority to evict someone at any time, for a large variety of reasons. I thought I'd come up with an excellent lease, but I was wrong. All the horror stories included in this chapter occurred early on in my career; they're perfect examples of what can happen when you don't have an effective lease, or are unwilling to enforce it. Fortunately, I learned from each incident, did some research (i.e. contacted knowledgeable state and local authorities), and kept tweaking my lease as time went on.

If all the possible negative scenarios aren't addressed in your lease agreement, you may find yourself stuck with nasty situations, no easy solutions, and that burnout issue lurking just around the corner. What I've ended up with is a combination of three or four different leases. I use a longer, more involved lease for some of the higher-end properties I manage for other people. (I'm including it in Chapter 11.) But the lease I use for my own properties is short and simple to read. Lengthy, wordy leases filled with what I call "legalese" cause the tenant's eyes to glaze over after two or three paragraphs. You lose them before you get to the second page. Keeping it simple is, again, your best bet.

Note: This lease works very well in my jurisdiction. As with all forms contained in this or any other book, don't make the mistake of assuming my lease will be appropriate for your area. Check your local and state ordinances before going forward. But feel free to use and tweak this lease as needed.

Here's a copy of my airtight lease.

LEASE AGREEMENT

Month-to month rental agreement for _____ between
(address)

Barnes Properties and_____. Rent
is_____per_____ payable in advance, and the deposit is
_____. Please give 30-day notice upon moving.

Only the following people are to live here: _____

_____

Tenants agree to the following:

1) Has inspected the apt. and found it to be in safe, clean and rentable condition.
2) Keep the apt. and yard clean, mow grass, shovel snow when needed.
3) Keep music, TV, and other noise low so neighbors aren't bothered.
4) Make no changes (painting, etc.) without landlord's written permission.
5) No parking on the grass, and no vehicle repairs that will take more than one day.
6) Allow property manager to show or inspect apt. at reasonable times.
7) No pets.
8) No water-filled furniture.
9) Pay rent by check or money order, mailed no later than one day after due date. Late fee is $25. Keep your money order receipt as proof of payment. Eviction is filed if rent is more than five days late.
10) Tenants pay for any damage caused by them or their guests. You may call me to get the repair done.
11) Tenant will pay the following utilities: _____. For those who do not pay electric bills, $5 extra per week will be charged if a window air conditioner is being used.
12) No illegal activities on the premises.

13) We have insurance on the building, but not on your possessions. We recommend you obtain renter's insurance to cover your belongings.
14) Tenant will replace smoke alarm battery when needed.
15) Tenant will not sublease property without landlord's written permission.
16) $20 immediate fee if we have to come unlock your door (stolen/lost/forgotten key).
17) Tenant will not hold landlord or Barnes Properties liable for any accident or injury on the property, assuming negligence is not involved.
18) Barnes Properties has the right to evict you if you do not follow the rules of this lease. We will recover attorney fees, court costs and any other expenses involved. Tenants and their possessions may be removed at their own expense.

Special provisions_____ I/we understand the contents of this lease and agree to follow its rules as stated.
Tenant_____Date_____
Owner _____
Barnes Properties, (address here)
Property Manager, Barb xxx-xxx-xxxx home & fax xxx-xxx-xxxx cell

I've tweaked this lease several times through the years, and feel that all the negative tenant-caused situations are prohibited by the terms of the agreement. I had my real estate attorney read through it carefully, and the brevity of it astounded him. However, he found it to be very thorough and gave it his seal of approval for use in our jurisdiction. I'd like to review it with you point by point.

The first section lays out the general terms of the lease, i.e. house address, lessor/lessee names, rental amount, deposit, and length of lease. For most of my tenants, month-to month rental agreements are most appropriate. Why not yearly leases? Yearlong leases aren't realistic, because people move around quite a bit these days, and events occur that precipitate a change in living situations. Forcing my tenants to sign a year lease is a useless endeavor, not worth the hassle. A monthly or even six-month lease makes more sense in today's highly mobile world. Applicants are pleased to find out the lease is on a monthly basis, and are often willing to pay a little higher rent for the convenience. Also, the month-to-month lease allows me to make changes within the agreement, as long as I give the tenants notice of the change, a month in advance. I do ask them to give me a month's notice if they're moving, and most of the time they honor that request.

Some of my tenants prefer to pay their rent weekly if their job pays them weekly. If they had to pay monthly, they might struggle to come up with the entire amount, so I'm happy to oblige, in order to get paid on time. (Show me the money!) Actually, when a tenant rents one of my apartments for $125/week, I'm getting more than $500/month for that apartment. The rent, $125, times 52 weeks per year, divided by 12 months, equals about $542/month. The extra $42 is a nice bonus for having to put up with the extra work of weekly rent. That amount on a $150/week apartment is $650/month instead of $600. It's wise to be flexible with your tenants, allowing them their best shot at getting their rent paid on time, whether it's weekly or monthly.

Regardless of whether my people pay weekly, bi-weekly or monthly, I've been able to make my life and theirs easier by providing them with envelopes that have been addressed and stamped. This idea was definitely one of my most brilliant brainstorms. It eliminates the "I didn't have a stamp" or "I didn't have an envelope" excuse. This plan also saves me time and gasoline.

The deposit should be at least enough to cover the amount of rent you'd lose between the day you file eviction and the day the court orders them to vacate, which for me is about three weeks. Although higher-end properties usually draw a full month's rent as a deposit, this may be a little steep for some people. Your local small claims court can give you eviction information, so that you can charge a deposit that will cover you in the event you have to kick someone to the curb. By the way, deposits aren't income, so don't record them as such. You're merely holding that money until some future date when your tenant moves out. The deposit may become income at that point, when you apply it to late rent or move-out costs, etc. Again, check your local, landlord/tenant ordinances to find out how to handle deposit monies, or ask your real estate attorney.

For non-eviction-related moves, my tenants may get some or all of the deposit returned to them, depending on the condition of the apartment. It's wise to be very specific about refund requirements. Upon move-in, you may want to provide the tenant with a list of costs involved (i.e. carpet shampooing, painting, cleaning, etc.) on the other end, when they move out. These monies may be deducted from the deposit, if the condition of the apartment doesn't meet your satisfaction.

Tenants agree to the following:

1) Has inspected the apt. and found it to be in safe, clean and rentable condition. This is what I call the "What you see is what you get" clause. Marco looked at my apartment on a stifling July afternoon. Although I allow tenants to install window units, only a few of my rentals have central air. After screening and renting the apartment to him, Marco started whining about the heat. He wanted me to install central air, or give him a window unit. I reminded him that he'd agreed to accept the apt as is when he moved in, and he reluctantly bought his own window air conditioner.

2) Keep the apt. and yard clean, mow grass, shovel snow when needed. This is one of the most important points of my lease. Early on, I'd neglected to add the "keep the apt. clean" clause, and boy, did I pay for *that* omission. Gary had gotten behind in his rent payment for the third time, and I wasn't willing to let him slide anymore. It was time for us to go our separate ways, but I wanted to make it painless for both of us if I could. He agreed to my two-part bribe.

"Gary, if you're out by Sunday night and leave the place clean and empty, I won't file eviction on Monday."

I drove around back of the duplex and let myself in through the kitchen. Upon entering, I discovered he'd only followed through on *half* the bribe. Gary was gone. Gary's clothes and personal items were gone. Evidently, he'd had a little trouble with the "clean and empty" part. I'd been in this kitchen six weeks earlier and it was in decent condition. But now...

I was greeted by a busy little swarm of deliriously happy fruit flies. Fifty or sixty of them hovered above the stove. Numerous sheets of flattened-out, food-encrusted aluminum foil were stacked neatly on the stovetop. The pile was about two feet high. Another team of fruit flies circled eight or nine open garbage bags that reeked of rancid meat and rotten fruit. Lovely combo. I summoned the nerve to open the refrigerator door, startling another huge colony of fruit flies inside. (How'd they get in *there?*) Black and green fuzz adorned a half-eaten chicken. I noticed a plastic gallon of milk stamped with a date that expired six months ago. The plastic milk jug was *swollen,* prompting me to think it could blow at any moment. Some downright scary-looking foods in various stages of decay peeked through several wads of crimped aluminum foil scattered throughout the shelves. I shut the door, stepped over the open garbage bags, and left the kitchen. After a quick trip to my car, I returned to the scene of the grime, armed with 55-gallon trash bags and rubber gloves.

This story (and others like it...I'm a slow learner) taught me two things. First, put a clean apt. clause in the lease. Second, get inside and do periodic checks on the apartments. Today, when I encounter an abused apartment, I leave a threatening note, stating I'll return in a couple days to reinspect the apartment. Eviction will be filed if the problem hasn't been totally corrected. Incidentally, it doesn't hurt to take photos of nasty, eviction-worthy situations. I've never been challenged, but it's always smart to cover yourself.

Check out the photograph below. This is Ruby's apartment. When I went in to do my first apartment check on her, I was totally overwhelmed by the clutter. But like the old saying goes, one person's trash is another person's treasure. Obviously, Ruby loved collecting all kinds of knickknacks. She was particularly fond of watermelons and plastic flowers. Initially, I was stunned by this scene. But upon closer inspection, I found that her home was actually clean under all the knickknacks and wall art. So when you do your apartment checks, you must be able to look beyond people's decorative tastes and discern whether they're keeping your home clean underneath it all.

I don't enjoy doing yard work at my own house, let alone my rentals, so mowing the grass is the responsibility of the tenants. Initially, I bartered this job with Barry, one of my tenants. He was a thirty-year-old construction worker whose protruding belly attested to his fondness for Budweiser, so I'd buy him a case now and then, in return for his mowing the grass where he lived. If he was out when I delivered, I'd just let myself in and leave the beer on the kitchen counter. On one such occasion when he didn't answer the door, I came on in and walked toward the kitchen with the beer. A muffled sound to my right startled me, so I looked in that direction. There lay the snoring Barry, sprawled on the bed, *stark naked*. I quickly backpedaled to the front door and left the beer inside. Since that day, when I enter someone's apartment, I call out loudly to announce my presence instead of assuming no one's home.

I'd like to add a few words here about bartering. The words are

"Just say no!" The only person I barter with these days is Craig. He does maintenance work and rents an apartment from me. We occasionally barter rent for his hours of maintenance work, and it's a wonderful relationship for both of us. Aside from him, I barter with no one. Also, I'd witnessed the quality of his work before entering into the barter situation with him. If you do decide to barter with someone, know the level of his or her expertise before entering into the agreement. Many times, tenants want to do some kind of work in return for deposit money or rent. Believe me, it's not worth making any deals that are going to rob you of the money you deserve. I usually tell them the work is my job as the property manager (remember, they don't realize I'm the owner), and that I need the income it brings.

Shoveling snow, like mowing, is a shared job between the tenants. It's their responsibility, and if they don't want to do it, they can always pay a neighborhood kid to do it for them. If the grass gets long and mangy-looking, I leave a threatening note and a time frame in which it needs to be done. If your tenants are remiss about keeping the exterior of the property in good condition, it's you who will receive a letter from the Board of Health, threatening a citation or court appearance. The fines and penalties for violations can be substantial, so it's important to be attentive to the exterior of your properties. I got a letter from the Board of Health regarding the back yard in the picture below. Maggie's front yard looked okay, albeit a little cluttered. I should've checked the back before it got this bad. Fortunately, she cleaned it up in the time allotted by the authorities. Tall grass and weeds, trash strewn about, hanging gutters, broken windows, inoperable vehicles, old appliances on porches, rickety garages, etc…these situations are citations waiting to happen.

3) Keep music, TV, and other noise low so neighbors aren't bothered. I've had to evict people for playing music too loud, fighting with their friends or family members, and other obnoxious behavior. Upon move-in, I make it clear they need to be considerate of their neighbors in the adjoining apartment, and one warning is sufficient. If the police are summoned, I usually file eviction. With all cases of lease violations where you're issuing a warning, make sure it's in writing, and keep a copy for yourself. I've never had a person try to fight me on this, but it's a good idea to cover your bases, in case you need to support your action.

4) Make no changes (painting, etc.) without landlord's written permission. Another thing I learned the hard way. My forty-year-old tenant decided he'd give his apartment a face-lift, and repainted the entire apartment one weekend. He loved the results, told me it looked more like a bachelor pad now, and encouraged me to come take a look. I feared the worst, with good reason. The dining room was bright aqua, the bedroom was muddy brown, and the kitchen was yellow-orange with a shocking green rooster-adorned border pasted haphazardly along the ceiling. He was so proud. I was so appalled. He wasn't even a good painter; he'd slopped paint all over the baseboards, drips had gotten on the carpet, and he'd bumped the ceilings several times as well. Even if a tenant gets your okay on the color, you can't trust they'll do a decent job of it, so don't go there at all. Sometimes tenants will want to change out the window coverings, which is okay if they save the originals and give them to me.

Satellite dishes are an issue I've had to deal with quite a bit. Most of the time, tenants have these installed on the roof, siding or in the yard without consulting me first. I don't want to deny them access to satellite TV, but don't want to have my houses or yards cluttered up with that stuff when the tenant moves out, either. The least destructive choice is the yard instead of anywhere on the house or roof, and I make them sign a contract stating they'll remove the dish if they move out.

After being out of town for the weekend, I returned to find that someone had done some unauthorized work at one of my rentals. When I left town, it was a cute little duplex, with white siding and dark brown trim. When I returned, half the trim had been painted (again, sloppily) bright neon yellow! My tenants hadn't done it; they figured I'd arranged to have it done. I assume whoever began the job realized, halfway through, they had the wrong address. Their mistake cost me several hundred dollars, and I never found the culprits. I guess that was a "no changes" issue I couldn't have prevented.

5) No parking on the grass, and no vehicle repairs that will take more than one day. For some reason, people decide it's okay to park in back of the house, not on the alley, but right up in back of the house, like maybe two feet from the back door. This tears up the grass, makes a muddy mess when it's wet outside, and just looks bad. Most of my homes have street parking out in front, and with several of them, I've provided space for two more cars in the back, by trucking in some #53 packing gravel. As you might imagine, spreading that gravel is a *really* fun job.

Inoperable cars up on blocks in back of the house are an easy target for the Board of Health, who'll send a notice threatening a fine if the car isn't removed. A notice will be sent if a vehicle doesn't have a license plate, has a flat tire, or is basically a wreck. You may think it's just the tenant's problem. Well, think again. It's your problem too. Fines and penalties are attributed to the party that causes the violation, and to the owner of the property. I try to make sure all vehicles at my properties are in good repair, so as not to attract the attention of city authorities. With a possible eviction looming if the tenants don't take care of the problem, they usually comply.

6) Allow property manager to show or inspect apt. at reasonable times. The key words here are "at reasonable times." This clause gives me the right to go in when I feel it's appropriate to do so. I don't abuse this privilege. For example, when I'm evicting someone, I may want to show the apartment to a potential tenant. Recently, I've incorporated random cleanliness checks into my schedule. At the end of every month, when I deliver envelopes to my tenants in which they can send the next month of rent, I include a tenant letter. In it, I'll mention that I may be coming around to check out the condition of the apartments within the next week or two. Tenants tend to do a better job of cleaning, etc. when they know that I may be stopping in to take a look. The incident with oddball Gary (and others like him) prompted me to include occasional inspections in my routine.

7) No pets. Some of my tenants have a hard enough time taking care of *themselves*, let alone a pet. Although I'm truly an animal lover, I've seen firsthand the havoc and destruction they can create at one of my apartments. I've had the no pets clause in my lease from the start, but I do make exceptions from time to time. Occasionally, a long-term, excellent tenant has asked me to allow a cat or dog. Knowing they're great tenants who are clean and responsible, I've granted them permission and haven't regretted it later. This can cause a problem, however, if the property's a duplex and the irresponsible next door neighbor asks me why he can't have a pet, too. Turtles, guinea pigs, hamsters, fish, reptiles and snakes are okay with me; they're confined to cages for the most part. But cats and dogs are a different story altogether.

A couple years ago, I'd filed eviction on a guy who inhabited an upstairs apartment and was late with his rent one time too many. The court ordered him out on a Friday, and because my daughter Anne was visiting me, I didn't get down there until Sunday. She came along, just for kicks. Well, she got more than she'd bargained for. Unbeknownst to me, my tenant had left several days prior, leaving an unauthorized pet cat behind, with no food, no water, and an overflowing litter box. When we let ourselves in, the stench was overwhelming. This poor cat had used the entire apartment as its litter box, and my new carpet was totally trashed. Anne grabbed a broom as we tried to corner the cat to throw it out the door; at one point she about had it trapped. It was then that I had a brief but costly dumbass attack. I decided I was quick enough to grab the cat by the scruff of its neck and throw it out the door. Bad decision. As I grabbed the scruff, the cat sank its teeth into the back of my hand and didn't let go. I carried him to the door and tossed him out, but my hand was bleeding and immediately started to swell. A twenty-four hour stay in the hospital on continuous I.V. antibiotics, and minor surgery on my hand to debreed it taught me (the hard way) that you don't mess with cats. Or dogs, for that matter. From that day forward, when confronted with a difficult pet situation, a call to Animal Control became my solution of choice.

If you decide to allow pets, make sure you protect yourself by charging a hefty non-refundable pet deposit, or charge a higher rent payment for the privilege of having the pet. Also, have them sign a pet agreement like the one I'm including here.

PET AGREEMENT

This agreement is part of the lease for _____
dated_____.

Tenants want to keep a_____named_____in the dwelling. They agree to:

1) Keep the pet under control at all times and to not leave the pet unattended for an unreasonable amount of time.

2) Keep the pet (if a dog) fenced or tethered when outdoors unattended

3) Make sure the pet does not become unnecessarily noisy or aggressive with neighbors.

4) Provide the pet with regular health care, and to have the pet neutered/declawed within the first six/seven months.

5) Pay_____per_____for the privilege for having the pet.

Tenants agree that this agreement applies only to the pet mentioned above.
Tenants agree that the Owner has the right to revoke permission to keep the pet if the tenants break this agreement.

Signed,

_____ (Owner)

_____ (Tenant)

6) No water-filled furniture. Although waterbeds are somewhat outdated, I still encounter them from time to time. You can certainly make the tenant sign a paper stating they'll take care of any damage caused by the presence of that waterbed, but it's much easier to just say no.

7) Pay rent by check or money order, mailed no later than one day after the due date. Late fee is $25. Keep your money order receipt as proof of payment. Eviction is filed if rent is more than five days late. Some of my tenants don't have checking accounts; they pay all their bills with money orders, which in my opinion is preferable to a check. Checks bounce. Money orders don't. If someone writes a bad check, it's several days before your bank notifies you, so you lose precious time while you try to collect the money or file eviction. When tenants get behind in their rent, I look at their big picture before jumping into the eviction process. Have they often been late? Did they make it up quickly? Are they clean and honest people? If the tenant's big picture is shaky, I don't waste time and money trying to let them get caught up in their rent.

My sister Margo owns rental properties, higher-end than mine. Her tenants are solid upper-middle-income people who pay their rent by the month. She's installed lock boxes at each of her properties. The box has a slot into which her tenants deposit the rent. One key opens all the boxes, and she stops by on the fifth of each month to collect the rents. Recently, someone broke into one of her boxes and stole all the rent checks and money orders. She's now upgrading her locks to prevent another break-in, and is going to post a "no cash inside" sign on each box. The lock box is an alternative to having tenants mail their rent payments, but you'll need to make sure the box is tamper-proof if you go with this option.

Rent is generally due on Friday, for my tenants who pay by the week. I give each family, at the end of the month, four or five pre-addressed, stamped envelopes so they can send the next month's rent to me on time, no excuses. The rent usually appears in my post office box no later than Wednesday of the following week. Thursday, then, is what I call kick-ass Thursday. On Thursday, I deliver my Notice to Pay Rent or Quit form letter, which I'm including here. It looks very official, and prompts a quick response by the tenant. For my monthly tenants, I deliver it on the fourth day of the month. Sometimes, they'll have already sent the rent, and if they can produce the money order receipt, they're off the hook. More often than not, the money hasn't been sent and the tenant is faced with paying the rent plus the late fee. Again, you must look at their tenant history with you, and determine whether or not to file eviction.

NOTICE TO PAY RENT OR QUIT

TO_____

and all other tenants in possession of the premises described as:

ADDRESS_____

Please take notice that the rent is now due and payable on the above-described premises which you currently occupy.

Your rental account is delinquent in the amount itemized as follows:

Rental period_____Rent due_____
Rental period_____Rent due_____

Total Rent due_____
Late fee_____

Total Balance Due_____

You are hereby required to pay said rent IN FULL within _____ days or to REMOVE FROM AND DELIVER UP POSSESSION OF THE ABOVE-DESCRIBED PREMISES, OR LEGAL PROCEEDINGS WILL BE INSTITUTED AGAINST YOU to recover possession of said premises, to declare the forfeiture of the Lease under which you occupy said premises and to recover rents and damages, together with court costs and attorney's fees, according to the terms of your Lease Agreement.

Please contact me immediately to arrange for payment to be made.

Dated this_____day of_____, 20_____.

10) Tenants pay for any damage caused by them or their guests. You may call me to have the repair done. Sometimes tenants don't want to admit they've damaged something in the apartment, so I don't get a call. When I do my periodic checks inside, I always ask them if everything's working okay. If they've broken a window, for instance, I have Craig replace it with plexi-glass (more durable than regular glass) and I inform the tenant what the cost will be. They add it into their next rent payment. Sometimes they volunteer to do the repair themselves, but I've learned the hard way that things may end up in worse shape than before if the tenant does the repair.

11) Tenant will pay the following utilities: _____ . For those who do not pay electric bills, $5 extra per week will be charged if a window air conditioner is being used. At my single-family properties, the tenant is responsible for all utility payments. This is one of the nice advantages of owning single-family rentals. With my duplexes and triplexes, the situation varies. I pay the water bill at all my multi-family properties; the water is never metered separately. Of my twenty-nine units, only eight of them have their own gas meters. Most of the units are metered separately for electricity. A few of my duplexes have the water, electricity and gas each on one meter, making it impossible for the tenant to pay *any* of their own utilities. When this is the case, I determine a monthly average for each of these bills, and I fold it into the weekly or monthly rent payment. Actually, many of my tenants prefer to pay no utilities; they'd rather have only one payment per week. And in some cases, they have outstanding bills with the utility companies, so they're unable to put the account in their name. In these cases, I make them pay a little more for the privilege of having me pay the bills. For example, if the monthly electric bill for their apartment averages $50 times 12 months divided by 52 weeks in a year = $11.54, I add $15 into their weekly rent payment. The worst thing you can do is pay the utilities for them and have it be a losing proposition for you! You should be rewarded for taking care of the bills for them by making a little extra money on the deal.

12) No illegal activities on the premises. A couple years ago, the tenants at my four-plex complained about cute little Tammy, a restaurant dishwasher, who had "friends" stopping by at all hours of the day and night. When there's lots of traffic in and out of an apartment, you need to suspect drug activity. I called the local police department and told them about the constant traffic at Tammy's apartment. They took it from there, sending undercover policemen to patrol the area at various times of day and night. Sure enough, a few days later they busted her and several of her friends. I had to go to the county courthouse to obtain the arrest report, which stated that eight people were arrested. A large quantity of crack cocaine was confiscated, along with six handguns. (Yikes!) Tammy went to jail and I went to court to file eviction. I got her out quickly. If you suspect illegal activity at one of your properties, contact authorities and keep your distance.

13) The owner has insurance on the building, but not on your possessions. We recommend you obtain renter's insurance to cover your belongings. The tenants need to know that if there's a fire at the house, their belongings are not protected by the owner's insurance. I recommend they buy renters' insurance, which is inexpensive.

14) Tenant will replace the smoke alarm battery when needed. Before a new tenant moves in, I always make sure the smoke alarm is in working order. There should be one alarm per floor, and one in the basement. From the day they move in, they're responsible for changing out old batteries and putting in fresh ones. When you have an attorney look over your rental agreement, get input about any disclosure forms required by the federal, state or local government. For example, I'm required to have a lead-base paint disclosure, signed by my tenant and me. Other disclosures address water quality, mold issues, etc. Larger cities' landlord-related websites usually give details about the necessary disclosure forms and where to obtain them.

15) Tenant will not sublease property without landlord's written permission. I stopped by one of my apartments to do a routine check, and didn't recognize *any* of the people there. After a few moments of confusion, I was told my former tenant had moved to Mississippi and these people were taking over. (Great.) I whipped out an application and had them fill it out, because the apartment was spotless and they seemed responsible. I checked out the work references, allowed them to stay, and the replacements ended up being excellent tenants. I lucked out in this instance, but I decided to protect myself in the future by adding this clause to my lease.

16) $20 immediate fee if we have to come unlock your door (stolen/lost/forgotten key). I just recently added this clause. Tenants have been apologetic and willing to pay for the inconvenience when they lock themselves out or lose their key. But last month, I had someone knocking on Craig's door at 3 a.m. because she had left her key inside and locked herself out. He lives in the garage apartment behind her duplex. She refused to pay the fee, stating that it's part of his job, and nothing was written in the lease. I paid Craig the $20 and added this clause.

17) Tenant will not hold landlord or Barnes Properties responsible for any accident or injury that occurs on the property, assuming negligence isn't involved. In today's litigious world, we need to protect ourselves from fraudulent lawsuits. If one of your tenants falls down the steps in a drunken stupor and breaks a leg, it's not your fault. The negligence part of this clause would refer to steps that were rotten or had no railing, etc…in that case, his broken leg could be blamed on you.

18) Barnes Properties has the right to evict you if you do not follow the rules of this lease. We will recover attorney fees, court costs and any other expenses involved. Tenants and their possessions may be removed at their own expense. This is where I say something like, "We take excellent care of our homes and our tenants, but we also evict people quickly if they don't follow the terms of our lease. So, please make sure you understand everything in the agreement. Do you have any questions about the lease agreement?"

The "Special Provisions" section at the end of the lease allows for other issues that might come up. For example, I occasionally allow a pet on the premises. I indicate as much on this line, and attach a pet agreement to the lease. Or, if I've promised to replace the refrigerator, I'll note it here, along with a projected delivery date.

When my new tenants and I meet at the apartment, I bring two copies of the lease and go through it carefully with them. They sign both copies and keep one for themselves. My last comment goes something like this: "If you pay rent on time and keep your place clean, we'll all be happy." Late rent and filthy tenants constitute a large part of all lease violations, so I like to leave them with those parting reminders.

When you only have one rental property, it's easy to keep track of rent payments. But as your portfolio grows, you'll need to carry a rent collection sheet with you at all times. I use a 13-column ledger sheet, with my apartment units listed vertically on the left and the weeks/months across the top. Sometimes people want to pay ahead (halleluiah!) or pay when they see you, and it's important to have your rental sheet with you and record the payment immediately. Always provide them with a receipt if they pay in cash.

NONPAYING? GET 'EM OUT

Okay, so you've screened all the applicants and picked a winner. They rent the apartment, and everyone concerned hopes this will be a long and wonderful relationship. My longest tenancy has been several years. My shortest stay was by a girl named Leticia. We met at the apartment at 10:00a.m.. She was excited and had brought lots of her belongings in a pickup truck, ready to move in immediately. She called me at 2:00p.m. to tell me she was moving out. She'd seen a mouse. In at ten, out at two. (Sigh...)

No matter how hard you try to perfect your tenant selection process, a certain percentage of tenancies just don't work out. People have family crises that force them to move unexpectedly. They lose jobs. They split up with their significant other. They get laid off from their jobs. Their car breaks down and they can't get it fixed *and* pay the rent. They get sick and can't work. Hundreds of crises upset the stability in their lives and make it impossible to pay rent, and it's your job to try and coax them out of the apartment without having to spend time and money on filing eviction.

When everything falls apart and my tenants can't pay the rent, the first priority is to get them out quickly. If I'm there on kickass Thursday and they can't make up the missed week of rent on Friday, the handwriting's on the wall. They need to leave! I usually tell them that, if they can be out by the following Tuesday or Wednesday and leave the place spotless, I won't file eviction. This option is attractive to those who don't want an eviction on their personal record. In my area, I receive the same court date whether I file on kickass Thursday or on the following Wednesday, so I'm not losing any time by offering this option to them. If eviction is the best solution, it can be filed at your local small claims court. In my area, there's an $80 fee for filing.

I totally jump the gun on eviction when I'm dealing with a tenant who's been difficult in one way or another from the start. Like Paul, who lived with his girlfriend Sheila. While she worked, Paul hung out at home with his punk friends, smoking, drinking, watching TV and surfing porn sites on the computer. He didn't lift a finger to keep the apartment clean. He was too busy. When Sheila got laid off, I asked Paul if he was going to get a job to help out. His flippant response said it all. "I can't work. I have attention definite disorder." Huh?

Sometimes, in an effort to get someone out quickly, I'll offer a nice little bribe. "If you're out by the weekend and clean the place well, I'll give you back $100 of your deposit." Dangling this carrot works with some tenants. I figure it this way…if I can get rid of them quickly, I avoid losing at least two weeks of rent while we wait for the court date.

Early in my career, I got scammed more often than not. Being too softhearted and trusting doesn't work well in this business. There are people who'll look you in the eye and lie like there's no tomorrow. Wanting to believe the best in people, I lost thousands of dollars, choosing to believe they'd have the money in two days, or next week, or whenever. Don't be sucked in by these people. Although there are some really sad situations out there, it's *not your job* to fix things and counsel your tenants.

My nineteen-year-old tenant, Ashley, and her boyfriend had fallen behind on their rent. She'd been working as a waitress, and I guess business was slow. When I showed up to tell them I was filing for eviction the next day, she met me at the door with a happy smile on her freckled face. She bounced out onto the porch in a pink tube top, below which jiggled her plump, bare belly adorned by a rhinestone bellybutton jewel. She excitedly told me there'd be no more problems with the rent; she'd gotten a new job. When I asked for details, Ashley confided that she'd be stripping for a living, "but I don't have to take everything off". So sad. As a landlord, you can't fix situations. You have to deal with what *is*. You can't counsel tenants out of bad habits or past behaviors. You'll drive yourself crazy and lose money in the process.

I've come up with an alternative to letting people slide. I tell them the owner isn't willing to wait for the money, and he's having me file eviction today. However, if they can get the rent caught up before the court date, we'll let them stay. This is only if they've been decent tenants. If they're able to catch up on their rent, I also have them pay back the filing fee for the eviction, so that I'm not out any money.

Quite often, people will pack up (or *not* pack up) and leave if they know eviction is imminent. When tenants leave things behind, you need to:

1) Try to contact them through their work, a friend or a relative. Refer to your application to get these phone contacts.
2) Take pictures of what's been left in the apartment.
3) Check with an attorney about your legal rights, if you can't reach the tenant or other contact. Ask him/her what constitutes "abandoned property."

In the beginning, I worried about what to do with their belongings if they left furniture, etc. behind. The law in my state says the tenant's personal property is considered abandoned if "a reasonable person would conclude that the tenant has vacated the premises and has surrendered possession of the personal property." So I just use good judgment; most of the time it's pretty obvious. *If the clothing and decent items are gone, they're probably not planning on returning for the junk!* Another investor offered this solution:

"If anyone ever questions you about throwing out the trash left behind, tell them the tenant abandoned the property, thus forfeiting rights to the junk they left for you to clean up."

And most of the time, it is junk and trash. Again, check with an attorney about what constitutes abandoned property in your state. I always try to contact a friend or relative of the tenant and tell them I'm bagging the stuff up and putting it out for trash pickup. I've never had anyone come back at me for getting rid of the precious heirlooms they left in the apartment.

When I've filed the eviction and the tenant decides to stay until the court date, it's usually because they know the process and have been through it. They know they can stay another two weeks, not paying rent, waiting for the court date, and they also know the judge will let them stay for four days after the court appearance. Most of my tenants don't attend. They realize the outcome will be the same whether they show up or not. So in these cases, there's no option other than waiting it out, which is frustrating. But I don't worry about the things I can't control, and I concentrate on finding a better tenant next time. Check with your small claims court about the process and time frame in your area.

You must realize, a certain percent of vacancies is to be expected (see Diamond or Dud) and this is just part of the business. Beyond that, all you can do is be patient and know that another tenant will come along.

What do you do if the judge orders the tenant out by a certain date and they don't go? This has only happened to me once, but I need to discuss it here. You can check with your local small claims court to see what their procedure is in this instance, but I think it'll be similar to ours. The judge had ordered Janet and her alcoholic boyfriend Bobby, out. Their relationship had taken a downturn and so had the apartment. They didn't manage to leave on time, so the procedure here is to contact the sheriff through the small claims court, and a moving company as well. We all showed up at the apartment together. The sheriff was to remove the tenants, and the movers were to remove the tenants' belongings. If the tenants wanted to reclaim their things, they'd have to pay the moving company a fee. When I showed up that morning, the sheriff asked, "Are those your tenants?"

Sure enough, there they were, half way down the alley, dragging two bags of clothing behind them. The two bags were the *only* things they took from the apartment. What I didn't know is the moving company only takes items that can be resold, in case the tenants don't reclaim them. The movers took *three* items out of that apartment. And worse yet, I had to pay them $300 for the favor! I stuffed 28 huge trash bags with the rest of their junk, which consisted of filthy clothes, broken furniture, food-encrusted dishes, torn books and magazines, smelly shoes, a few used diapers, etc. There was a decent looking crock-pot on the counter, so I peeked inside. Big mistake. There was life inside and it was *moving*. Hundreds of whitish, slimy maggots had found a home. Fortunately, I've only had to call the sheriff and the moving company this one time, though I've done many evictions.

Admittedly, some of the stories contained in this chapter are truly scary and disgusting. Trust me, they don't occur on a weekly or monthly basis. I've included them for illustration and entertainment. Instituting apartment checks has saved me from facing scenarios like these. If I go into someone's apartment to check its condition, I always give advance notice of my visit, usually in my monthly tenant letter. After I've gone through the apartment, I leave a "good report" letter or a "bad report" letter, depending on the condition of the apartment. The people whose apartments are well maintained receive this letter:

Dear _____,

I stopped by your apartment today to do my routine cleanliness check, and I just wanted you to know your place looks great. We work hard to take good care of our homes and our tenants, and it's rewarding to come into someone's apartment and find it looking this nice.

Thank you so much for doing a great job of keeping things clean…I wish we had more tenants like you!

Have a good day,
Barb

People respond to a pat on the back, and should be thanked for keeping their apartments in good condition.

On the other hand, when I enter someone's apartment and it looks like a train wreck, I respond accordingly with a very different form letter. The underlying threat to this letter is eviction, and it's meant to whip them (and their apartment) into shape. Here it is:

Dear _____,

I stopped by today to do my routine cleanliness check of your apartment, and yours needs some help right now. In your lease, you agree to "keep yard and apartment clean." Everything was spotless when you moved in, but today I noticed the following areas need attention:

1) KITCHEN
SINK _____
DISHES_____
STOVE _____
POTS AND PANS _____
FLOOR_____

2) BATHROOM(S)
BATHTUB _____
SHOWER _____
SINK_____
TOILET _____
FLOOR_____

3) LIVING AREAS
GENERAL CONDITION _____
FLOORS_____

4) YARD AND GARBAGE AREAS
TRASH _____
YARD _____

ADDITIIONAL COMMENTS _____

THANKS FOR YOUR COOPERATION...WE APPRECIATE IT. I'LL BE BACK ON _____ TO DO A RE-CHECK OF THE APARTMENT. <u>PLEASE</u> <u>MAKE SURE THE ABOVE THINGS HAVE BEEN TAKEN CARE OF</u>. THANK YOU!

BARB XXX-XXX-XXXX

Doing these apartment checks is not easy. I keep my house a lot neater than some of my tenants do, but much of what I see there is just clutter, not filth. You have to be able to look beyond the clutter and determine whether they're totally letting the place go or cleaning it on a regular basis. Are you sticking to the kitchen floor? Is the inside of the toilet a little scary? (You know what I mean...) Is there scum around the inside of the tub? Dirty dishes that have been in the sink for days? Could you write your name in the grease on the stovetop? These situations draw bugs and other undesirable pests, and must be addressed in your apartment checks. On occasion, I have to make a threat at the bottom of the sheet, casually mentioning the "e" word. Your tenants need to know you'll evict them for being filthy. If they know you mean business, they'll clean up their act. I've only had to evict a few tenants for this violation. By the way, if you do see the handwriting on the wall, keep a copy of your apartment check letter as documentation, just in case you need it in court.

A final word about evictions...when someone gets behind on the rent, move quickly. Trust them to get caught up, and make a written plan that each of you will sign. Or, if you have any doubt they can get caught up, file the eviction immediately. Going days, weeks or months with no income from that apartment is unnecessary. Get the nonpaying tenant out, and move on.

THE BOTTOM LINE

As I've said before, burnout is an issue in this business and most of the time, tenant management is the crux of the problem. As I stumbled through the early part of my landlording experience, I made countless rookie mistakes; some of the most appalling stories are chronicled in this chapter. Tenants took advantage of my kind and trusting nature. I believed every sob story, allowed them to stay too long (nonpaying), and lost thousands of dollars as a result. Through the years, I realized I'd best toughen up or give the management responsibilities to someone else. Paying a property manager 10-15% of rents seemed foolish. Why pay someone to do something I'm perfectly capable of doing myself? Not wanting to share the money, I toughened up. After years of trial and error--lots of error--I started reworking my lease. I was sick of wasting time and losing money.

Although I still treat my tenants with kindness and respect, I do enforce the rules of my lease. The result? Less hassle and frustration, and lots more money in my pocket. There's no need to allow tenant issues to drive you crazy or drive you out of a good, moneymaking career.

The cure for burnout can be found in this chapter. My airtight lease covers every sticky situation you'll face. Feel free to use any or all parts of it as you create your own lease that fits your personality and jurisdiction. If you're willing to enforce its rules, you'll save yourself time, money and frustration. And the "b" word won't be part of your vocabulary.

CHAPTER NINE
MAINTAINING THE APARTMENT

IN A PERFECT WORLD, once you get the apartment rented, you sit back and enjoy the fruits of your labor. Everyone pays on time and keeps their apartment/yard spotless and no one calls you on Friday night at 10:30 to tell you their toilet has overflowed, twice. Seriously though, if you've done a careful job of fixing up the place, you shouldn't have many calls from tenants having problems with the apartment. Beyond that, however, you'll need to take care of some general maintenance chores throughout the year.

EXTERIORS

Almost all of my rentals have bushes, trees, weeds, etc. that require my attention about twice a year. Armed with my saw and pruners, a Black & Decker™ lightweight gas-powered hedge trimmer (20 inch blade), Ortho Season-Long Grass and Weed Killer™, and my 55 gallon trash bags, I choose cool spring days and cool fall days to tackle the job as quickly as possible. Trimming trees and bushes really improves the curb appeal of the property, and although yard work is *not* my thing, I won't pay someone else to do what I can do myself. The end result is rewarding, too.

In every area of the country, there are nuisance plants and trees that choke out everything around them and cling to brick and vinyl siding, eventually damaging it. For example, ivy looks pretty, but you'll regret letting it creep up the side of your house. A couple of my rentals have extremely hardy poison ivy vines that spread along the ground as well as up stairways and siding. Because I've developed an allergy to it over the past couple years, my attire consists of long sleeves, long pants and gloves when I'm tackling poison ivy. I spray it with the Ortho product mentioned above, or cut through the stems at ground level, then come back in a few days to pull it out and bag it up. Whatever can't be pulled out can be killed with the spray. If your nuisance plants are bushes or trees, the easiest way to eliminate them is to cut them down as close to the ground as possible, and brush a thick coat of Ferti-lome Brush and Stump Killer™ onto the exposed areas. Sometimes it takes a follow-up application the next time I do my trimming, but this product is very effective. When nuisance plants are growing in a fence row, it's impossible to cut them down to ground level, so I trim back what I can and apply the stump killer.

It's wise to hire a tree-trimming company to cut back tree limbs that over hang your roofs and gutters. Limbs that break off can damage roofs and siding, and leaves will clog gutters and downspouts. The cost of the trimming is minimal compared to what you'll have to pay in damages if you let it go.

If the home has a working fireplace, have it checked yearly. Birds try to nest in chimneys, blocking the flue. A chimney cap will prevent this problem. Creosote forms on the inside walls, which can cause a chimney fire. Hire a qualified professional to clean and check your chimney.

Gravel parking is another exterior job that, if done right the first time, shouldn't require much tending. Measure the length and width of the area, and buy heavy plastic sheeting to lie over the entire area, so that grass and weeds won't poke through when you've laid the gravel. When you call to have the stone delivered, tell them you need #53 packing, and that it needs to be three or four inches deep. They'll figure out how much you need. Be aware of any power lines that cross the area you're covering; low-hanging lines will force them to use a smaller dump truck for the delivery. Adding gravel at some of my houses has helped alleviate problems caused by inadequate street parking, or tenants parking on the grass in back of the house. When I have gravel delivered, I try to make sure my kids and their boyfriends are around......Spreading it with a steel rake and shovel is backbreaking work, and I offer excellent bribes (mainly food related) if they're willing to participate. Fortunately, the gravel will look good for several years, and if you need to add to it, the second spreading requires less material and manpower.

When I'm doing my cutting and trimming chores, I also check the gutters and downspouts to make sure they're in good working order. Trays under the downspouts will help channel water away from the foundation.

Foundations are another item on my exterior checklist. Some foundations are brick, while others are stone or cement block. Regardless of the type of foundation on the home, it's a good idea to check it occasionally for cracks and crevices. Settling of the house will cause some shifting and cracking and although it's not a huge concern, the cracks should be filled so critters are denied access to the basement. The best solution is a foam product called Great Stuff™. It comes in a spray can, to which you attach a thin straw (provided) and it can fill even large cracks. It's wise to wear rubber gloves when applying Great Stuff, because 1) it's not water-soluble and 2) controlling the expansion of the foam takes a little practice. The first time I used this product, I inserted the straw into the crevice, and gave it a good squirt. Before I knew it, the foam totally filled the crevice, overflowed the opening, crawled down the foundation and onto the toe of my shoe. This stuff grows like crazy, so use it sparingly. It's light yellow, and can be painted after it dries. For cosmetic purposes, I usually paint my foundations (dark colors are best) if I've had to fill cracks. Otherwise, I leave them natural.

When tenants have moved out, there's usually a pile of trash out back. The heavy items such as couches, desks, etc. are picked up once a month by the city. Trash pickup is included with my sewage/water bill here. My city is currently giving out 96-gallon trash containers to every home or apartment, which will prevent hungry neighborhood dogs from scattering garbage across our yards and alleys. I'm thrilled about this addition, because garbage issues have been a nuisance from the start. If there are no leash laws in your area, animals *will* help themselves to your trash. Some of my tenants buy decent trashcans with lids, but many are content to put their bagged trash outside as is, which invites various animals to come over for a smorgasbord. Sprinkling the bags with ammonia will deter dinner guests, but most people won't remember to do it on a regular basis. I've sometimes provided good trashcans with tight-fitting lids, painting the apartment address on the side with spray paint. Some have been stolen, run over or otherwise damaged, and a few have lost their lids. But it seems smarter to try and alleviate the problem rather than deal with the aftermath of a canine buffet in the backyard.

Safety is a key issue with my rentals. When I walk around the house, I try to check for hazards that could result in my tenants getting hurt. Are the steps going up to the house in good repair? Is there a hand railing where there are more than three steps leading to a doorway? Are there low spots or holes in the yard that could cause someone to break an ankle? Do the storm doors have automatic closers that prevent them from slamming shut? Simple checking can save you a lot of trouble. Although I've never been sued, that possibility always lurks in the back of my mind and keeps me on my toes.

INTERIORS

When tenants move out, I get in there and work quickly; there's no sense in letting the apartment sit empty. Speed is of the essence in this business, and the quicker the turnaround, the quicker you're in the money again. Put your ad in the paper, but time it so the appearance of the ad coincides with the apartment being ready to show. You don't want applicants seeing the house before it's ready to rent.

I've streamlined my turnaround process by using a canvas tool caddy that holds most of the items I need every time I go in for a cleanout. I keep it stocked with these items:

Hammer	2 ½" trim brush
Tape measure	Glass cleaner
Phillips screwdriver	Five-in-one tool
Pen and notepad	Dish soap
Flat head screwdriver	Small putty knife
Paint can opener	Thin latex rubber gloves
Scrub brush with short stiff bristles	Barkeepers Friend
Dish cloth and hand towel	Utility knife
Paper towels	Krud Kutter
Scotch Brite™ dark green scrub pad	Dust brush
Small tube of Liquid Nails™ adhesive	

Repeated trips back and forth to the car are a waste of your time, and having a carryall with basic items in it saves time and effort. Other key items I have in my work car at all time

Small multi-purpose saw	Pest control weapons
Extra towels	Oven cleaner
Broom and dust pan	Extra locks
Shelf liner	Smoke alarm batteries
Mop	Pruners for shrubs and trees
Paint, stick, handle and roller sleeves	Thick gardening gloves
Shower curtains and rings	Large and small trash bags
All tenant keys	Appliance touch-up paint
Extension cord	Light bulbs
Spackle, drywall mud and drywall tape	Kilz spray paint
Tool box with assorted nails, screws	Radio/iPod
WD40™ and white lithium grease	

When tenants move out, I have them return the keys to the apartment. I keep a spare set of locks in my car (with keys) and install the spare set at the empty apartment. The set from the empty apartment then becomes the spare set that I keep in my car. Some of my apartments have one entry and some have two, so I have extras for each type of property. This trick saves me time and money in changing locks. Most doorknobs and deadbolts will last a few years, but over time, locks will stick a little bit and the key may not open the door easily. You can't expect your tenants to be patient with this situation. Their frustration may lead to the key breaking off in the lock, resulting in a 10:00 p.m. 911 call to you. A good remedy for locks that stick is a product called graphite powder. It's a dry powder that can be found at your home improvement store or hardware, and it'll loosen up the inside of the lock. I've heard WD40 recommended, but over time, it gums them up inside and shortens the life span of the lock. If you need to take your locks to a locksmith to have them rekeyed, the only parts you need to take are the parts into which you insert the key.

For interiors, a thorough inspection of the apartment should always be conducted. All the plumbing needs to be checked for leaks under sinks or around toilets, and the bath tub and shower should also be checked, to make sure the faucet and shower head are running smoothly. Always run water in the sinks and tub/shower, to see how well the drains are working. As a precautionary measure, you may want to use a drain-clearing product in all the drains, to clear out any grease or hair that may have accumulated. Sometimes a simple plunging will take care of a sluggish drain. Remember the toxic upholstery-eating product that ate right through the back seat of my car? It was 100% sulfuric acid and needless to say, I wouldn't recommend it. Since then I've found a product that's also very effective, called Roebic Drain Flow™. Although it's a sulfuric acid product, it's specially blended to produce less heat when used. The plastic bottle you'll find on the store shelf is encased in a thick plastic overwrap, providing a double barrier to the skin. Let that be a warning to you! Drain Flow is an excellent drain opener, but is a major irritant if it comes into contact with your skin. The smell of it alone will singe your nose hairs. When someone moves out, I treat all the drains simultaneously, because the acid's more effective that way. To reduce the splash factor, I always use a funnel to pour it slowly into the drains. Slow drains are a common problem, and doing this work myself saves me a lot of money in plumber visits. I store my Drain Flow in its own little plastic bucket, so that it won't tip and drip when being kept in my trunk.

When I go through the lease with new tenants, I always remind them to help keep their drains clear by 1) not allowing grease or food to go down the sink drain, and 2) using the toilet only for human waste and toilet paper. Too many times, I've paid someone to pull out all sorts of goodies from a clogged toilet drain. Paper towels, tampons and sanitary pads, hairpins, empty toilet paper rolls, toys, cotton balls, disposable razor heads, etc. When this happens, it's clearly the tenant's responsibility to pay for the drain clearing. However, if the property is multi-family, you're stuck. If the clog is in the main line, each tenant blames the other, and you can't prove anything.

A tenant had moved out and when I went in to paint, clean, etc., I was met by a horrible odor emanating from the bathroom. The sewer had backed up into the shower, below. It backed up with enough force to pop the center cap off the drain in the shower floor. My drain cleaning company came out immediately and cleared the line, which had clogged up mainly due to grease in the line. Many of my tenants cook with oil, butter or lard, and when the meal is done, they dump the remainder down the kitchen sink drain. It hardens in the sewer main line, and eventually, nothing can get through. The shower below was filled with over two inches of wet toilet paper and human waste. Ick! My five-in-one tool, Krud Kutter, Barkeeper's Friend and a stiff brush took care of it. The edges of this disaster area had dried by the time I discovered it, but the rest was a soupy mess. Humor gets me through rough situations…I called this "poop du jour."

Definitely a rubber glove job.

I recently stumbled on an excellent product that helps keep toilets clean. It's called Puricle 110 Never Scrub™ (like it already?), and it prevents scum, rust and hard water stains from building up on the inside of the toilet bowl. My own house is on a septic system, and I thought I'd try this product to see if it cut down on the rust and hard water stains. The results were amazing! You install the system inside the tank part of the toilet, and it's very easy to do. I hate cleaning the nasty stuff out of my apartment toilets, so now I'm using this system in the hood as well. Puricle can be reached at 1-866-757-0012, or more recently I've seen it sold at Wal-Mart under the name Kaboom Never Scrub™.

Don't overlook the basement when someone moves out. The furnace filter should probably be changed twice a year, and you'll want to make sure there are no water leaks that have occurred. I try to keep extra furnace filters in each basement, and encourage my tenants to change them on their own. Of course, they're more motivated to do this when they're the ones paying the heat bill, knowing a clean filter helps lower the cost of the heat.

I've had a few tenants choose the basement as their super-sized dumpster, tossing beer cans, poorly bagged garbage, and other trash down the steps. Sometimes it must feel like too much like work to bag it and carry it out to the trash can. I now include a peek into the basement during my apartment checks; if there's garbage or other litter present, a warning letter usually results in a cleanup of the situation.

Unlike the initial fix up, getting the apartment in rentable condition after someone leaves is usually a quick process. Only after long tenancies (or after heavy smokers) do I totally repaint. Most of the time, I can just touch up marks on the walls with some fresh paint. Where there are nail holes, you can take a swipe at them with spackle and a small putty knife, wipe off the excess with a damp cloth, and not even go over the spot with paint.

Depending on the tenant and length of tenancy, you'll want to shampoo the carpets. As I mentioned earlier, I own a lightweight carpet cleaner that works well. Hoover, Eureka and Bissell make good products for residential use. Oh, and our good friend, Krud Kutter, is an excellent substitute for carpet shampoo, which is very expensive. I use about a cup per gallon of hot water, and it does an incredible job. An alternative to owning your own carpet cleaning machine is Stanley Steemer. I've used them occasionally, and they always seem to be running specials. If the carpet's in good shape except for one or two unsightly stains and you're not ready to replace it, here's a little trick that'll get you through a couple more tenancies. Get a sturdy dinner plate and place it over the stain. Take your utility knife (use a new blade) and cut around the plate. Lift the stained circle of carpet out, and repeat the same process in a hidden area, like a closet. Take the unstained circle of carpet, place it where the stained circle used to be, and tack it down with small carpet nails. These will disappear in the nap of the carpet. Bingo! This is a quick fix that'll work if the colors of the old and new patches match well enough.

Maintaining the inside and outside of the rental isn't very time-consuming if you've done a decent job of fixing it up after you bought it. Just be thorough in your maintenance checks, because sometimes, your tenants won't tell you about problems, or they won't notice them.

WARM WEATHER PROBLEMS

The main problem I run into during the summer is lawn mowing not being done. Although I stress it when going through the lease with them, some tenants would rather stick their heads in the sand and pretend the grass isn't six inches long. Threatening eviction if the lawn isn't cut in a few days takes care of the problem. Be very specific on the time frame, and be willing to follow through. I've purchased a basic lawnmower, which I keep in my storage garage. On occasion, a duplex will be totally empty and the grass gets out of control, so it's nice to have the option of cutting it myself if I have to.

When a storm door doesn't have a screen, tenants sometimes just prop it open in the warm weather. Common sense would dictate differently, because all kinds of insects invite themselves into the apartment. I try to make sure the doors and windows have adjustable, if not permanent, screens to let the air in and keep the bugs out. Upon being caught with a pet cat or dog, I've had tenants say with wide-eyed innocence, "It got in through the open window and we can't get it to leave!" They think I was born yesterday.

I urge tenants to be careful when installing a window air conditioner, but sometimes they damage the windowsill or even crack the windowpane. These fix up costs belong to the tenant, of course.

Noise issues abound in the warm weather. Loud, annoying music, domestic arguments, screaming kids, you name it, and I've dealt with it. Fortunately, this and all the other problems associated with summer are covered in my airtight lease.

COLD WEATHER PROBLEMS

Cold weather presents its share of challenging situations. Most of my multi-family homes have only one thermostat, and various rooms tend to be warmer or cooler than others. In rooms that seem to get too much heat, I provide magnetic heat vent covers, which help divert the heat away from that room. If tenants have a room that's far enough away from the furnace that it doesn't get much warm air, I allow small space heaters to be used, if they're in good condition. (I have a couple that I lend out to people.)

Only six of my twenty-nine units are metered separately for heat; all the others are on one bill, and I pay it. When I embarked on my real estate career, I asked in my tenant letter that everyone keep their thermostats set at 72 degrees through the cold weather months. This was a futile effort on my part. Too many times, I'd pull up in front of a house and notice there were windows slightly open, and although the storm door was closed, the heavy front door would be wide open. When I knocked on the door, I'd be greeted by my tenant, who was perfectly comfortable in his T-shirt, shorts and bare feet. In the dead of winter. Something had to give; my gas bills were astronomical and people were cranking the thermostat up to 80 degrees so they could be comfy in the above attire. When I told my heating guy my tale of woe, he hit upon the solution-----Accustats™! He installed these in every apartment where I pay the heat bill. Now, there's no temperature dial on the thermostat, only an on/off switch. When it's on, the temperature goes to 72 degrees, which is quite generous of me, I might add. The gas company suggests 68 degrees, so if anyone complains, I remind them of that fact. And I remind them in the tenant letter that it is, indeed, wintertime, and dressing warmly is highly recommended.

Not too long ago, I received a 10:00 P.M. call from Georgia, complaining that her apartment was *freezing*. I asked her if she was dressing warmly and keeping her doors and windows shut, to which she snapped, "Of course! It's cold out! What do you think I am, crazy?" Georgia was a total whiner who managed to call or page me about insignificant issues on a regular basis. Since I'd learned not to take her too seriously, I didn't rush right down there. I called the other tenant, Rolando, to ask if his apartment was comfortable and he said yes. So, the next day I went to check out the situation. When I entered Georgia's apartment, it *did* feel cool. My small digital thermometer registered 64 degrees in her living room, which certainly indicated a problem somewhere. (It's good to have one of these thermometers in your bag of tricks, so that when tenants tell you it's too cold in their apartment, you can determine if there really is a problem.) Anyway, back to Georgia, who wasn't crying wolf after all. I touched the heat vents and could tell the heat hadn't kicked on recently. However, when I entered Rolando's apartment, it felt very comfortable! The thermostat was in the room next to the kitchen, and was indeed in the "on" position. When I walked into the kitchen, I discovered the source of the problem. All four burners on the electric stove were turned on high and glowing red, and the oven door was open, revealing the bright orange coils of an oven set to 450 degrees. It must have been 85 degrees in there. No wonder the furnace wasn't kicking on! This story prompted an addition to my next tenant letter, forbidding people to use their stoves as a heat source. Not only is it dangerous, it totally screws up the heat system for everyone else in the house.

If you live in an area where the temperature never dips down below 20 degrees (you lucky dog) you may skip this section. We're going to expound on freezing pipes, which can be a real headache for a landlord. When winter approaches, my tenant letter is full of great advice, including directions for keeping the water from freezing. I tell them if the temperature's going to be less than 20 degrees, they need to run a thin stream of hot and cold water from every faucet in the house, especially when the pipes are on an outside wall. It's also helpful to open the cabinet doors under each sink, so the warm air in the room can help keep those pipes warm. If they take my advice, they never have a problem. But every winter, I get calls from at least one tenant complaining about frozen pipes. It's difficult to muster up much sympathy, but I listen patiently. Usually, it's only one sink that's frozen, so it's not as if they're totally without water. Yes, they're inconvenienced, but if they run a small space heater on the floor in front of the sink cabinet for awhile, the pipes slowly thaw. A hair dryer can be used in the absence of a space heater. Home improvement stores sell styrofoam jackets that can be cut into various lengths and wrapped around pipes, but since I've not used them, I can't comment on their efficacy.

Although frozen pipes are a nuisance, they rarely burst. I did have one occasion where the pipes in Tamika and Shawn's apartment froze and they never called me about it. *Three days later* Tamika called and said she thought she'd been hearing water running. (Red flag.) She had no idea where the sound was coming from and I went there to check things out immediately. Yes, the pipes had frozen. Yes, they burst. The pipe in the cellar was gushing water at an unbelievable rate; the dirt floor was about eight inches deep in water. I had Craig come and turn the water off at the main until my plumber could get there. It didn't cost me lots of money to replace the broken pipe, but it really hurt my wallet when I had to pay the $350 water bill that resulted! Fortunately, the water company here makes adjustments on bills when pipes break. Something as minute as a running toilet can cause a water bill to spike, but again, our water company will adjust the bill down if you've made the repair.

I always encourage my tenants to call me if they have a problem at the apartment, but I've found that some people will avoid calling the landlord at any cost. Shawn and Tamika chose to suffer through three days without water instead of calling me about it. And I'm an approachable landlord! Go figure.

MAKING YOUR TENANTS BEHAVE

You'll find that some of your renters tend to get lazy, slack off and pull things over on you if you don't keep abreast of what is going on in and around their apartments. So how can you make them behave responsibly? By using threats and bribery, of course. We all try to avoid unpleasant consequences, and we all enjoy payoffs for good behavior.

Your airtight lease will coax your tenants to behave, or else. Also, the end-of-the-month tenant letter can address seasonal problems and other oversights of your tenants. Reminders are essential to include in each letter. Mowing grass, paying rent on time to avoid late fees, respecting the other tenant by keeping noise low, keeping the yard and apartment clean…. it's important to let them know you're on top of things. Also, your periodic checks of the interiors are essential if you want to avoid unpleasant surprises when someone moves out. I have several trusted tenants that don't require any monitoring (it's a beautiful thing), and the challenge is to fill all the apartments with that kind of tenant.

When Christmas rolls around, I deliver little gifts to all my tenants.

They usually consist of food items the tenants would consider a real treat, like fancy cookies, cakes or other dessert items. I rank my tenants and give gifts according to how easy they've been to manage. Your best tenants deserve recognition and rewards for being your best tenants, and you don't want to lose them. Showing your appreciation in small ways can make a big difference.

My main thrust in the November tenant letter is cautioning the tenants about overspending at Christmas. I warn them that we tend to file lots of evictions in January and February because people have overspent and don't take care of the rent payment. I remind them that one of their most precious possessions is the roof over their head, and ask them to take care of their rent first, and extras later.

Every time I have a vacancy, I look at the possibility of raising the rent at that unit. How do you know whether it's time to raise rent?

1) Check the For Rent ads in the local paper. If comparable apartments are going for higher prices, you're selling yourself short. When someone looks at one of my units and says, "Wow, this is a lot nicer than everything else I looked at for this kind of money," I know I haven't done my homework. I should've been asking more.

2) Look at some of the For Rent signs you see in your neighborhood. If the houses look comparable to yours, write down the number and call for information about the rental. If the apartment's a two bedroom that sounds similar to yours, but they're asking a lot more, you need to raise your price.

REWARDING YOURSELF (VERY IMPORTANT)

Being in business for yourself is one of those good news, bad news things. The good news is, you're the CEO, CFO, and project manager. The bad news is, you're the CEO, CFO, and project manager. The good news is, you *get* to run the show and make all the decisions. The bad news is, you *have* to run the show and make all the decisions.

I like being able to plan my schedule, and I keep good lists of what needs to be accomplished on a daily and weekly basis. Even if I have 100% occupancy (which doesn't last for long), there are always non-tenant-related chores, updates, paperwork, etc. that are staring at me, begging for my attention. And therein lies the downside to working for yourself. You can work ten-hour days, nights, and every weekend if that's the way you want to live. So, if you lean more toward the Type A personality, you need to be aware of this pitfall. Remember what they say about all work and no play. I have a strong work ethic, but my play ethic is right up there, too. I truly enjoy my work, but I take time to reward myself for my efforts. How do you balance it all?

For me, knowing my tenants can contact me at any time is essential for my peace of mind. My cell phone is the ironclad umbilical cord that keeps me tied to my tenants 24-7, and I'm fine with that. Knowing I can be reached in an emergency is all I need. Of course I get calls at inconvenient times, but that's part of the deal when you run your own business. I'm very active socially, and having the cell phone doesn't keep me from having a blast when I go out. Instead of taking every call when it occurs, I check the phone periodically and return calls that need my immediate attention. (Even with twenty-nine units, there aren't many calls that require immediate attention.)

Vacations are a deserved break from the job, and I make it a habit to get away quite a bit, for long weekends or, occasionally, an entire week at a time. Again, not a problem. Unlike some obsessive business people who allow vacation time to be disrupted continually by the phone, I keep mine turned off except when I choose to check and return messages. If you're going to conduct business the entire time you're away, *why go away?*

Whether I'm home or away, in the event an emergency occurs and I can't be reached immediately, Craig is my backup. It's not often that Craig has to be summoned when I'm away, but when he does, he just charges me his normal hourly fee. In return, I try to give him perks throughout the year. After all, he represents peace of mind for me while I'm off playing. I deserve the vacation, and he deserves the perks as his reward.

So, my advice would be to work hard, and play hard. If you're too geared toward the work side of life, you'll get burned out. Neglecting your need for relaxation will *guarantee* that burnout. Achieving a comfortable balance between work and play is essential to my well being, and finding the balance in your own life is a priority that should never be ignored.

THE BOTTOM LINE

Once you've gotten your rental fixed up and rented, you should be able to sit back and relax a little. If you do a good job on the rehab, repairs should be minimal. If you stick to the airtight lease, tenant issues won't drive you crazy.

It's important to let your tenants know you care about them and the house in which they live; touch base with them through occasional visits/apartments checks. Be aware of weather-related issues that accompany your rentals and address them in your tenant letters.

If you keep an eye on things you'll be rewarded in many ways: tenants who adhere to the lease, longer-lasting paint jobs, carpet, cabinets and appliances, less work when someone moves out and less money doled out for repairs.

After a few years of doing this business, you'll see that most things are routine, and most problems you encounter are just variations of a problem you've already dealt with in the past. There'll be few setbacks and few nerve-wracking surprises. If you have a quality person to run the show in your absence, you can take whatever personal time you desire. Being the CEO, CFO, COO, and project manager is hard work, but there are a multitude of perks and rewards attached to the job, and you need to take advantage of them. And the best reward of all? An owner who has minimum stress, maximum money in his/her pocket, and more free time in which to enjoy this life. That owner can be you.

CHAPTER TEN
PESTS
(INCLUDING THE TWO-LEGGED VARIETY)

AFTER CONDUCTING AN APARTMENT check, I'd evicted the filthy people who were living in their roach-infested apartment. When I entered the apartment after they moved, I was greeted by hundreds of cockroach family members (babies, teenagers, moms and dads, even grandmas and grandpas) who didn't even bother to skitter away when I came in. Just being in that apartment gave me the creeps. I was furious, and marched off to my local home improvement store to buy several bombs. Armed and dangerous, I returned to the apartment and placed a bomb in each room.

Before setting them off, I noticed the living room had a drop ceiling. I had a stroke of genius when I figured out that, if I got my ladder and moved one or two of the ceiling tiles aside, the fumes would permeate the space above the tiles as well as the room below. Wanting to be thorough, I ran out to get my ladder. That stroke of genius was actually a dumbass attack in disguise. When I reached up and carefully moved one of the ceiling tiles to the side, two huge roaches fell onto my hair. I shrieked, swiped at my hair with both hands, fell/jumped off the ladder backwards, and landed on my butt. The roaches panicked and ran. Too bad I don't have that episode on video…it was actually pretty hilarious. The bombs worked, sort of. There were fifty or sixty bodies when I returned the next day, but hundreds more had somehow avoided the wrath of the bomb. Surely, there had to be a better way.

Pest control can be challenging if you don't know what products to use, or if you're constantly paying a pest control service to do it for you. I came up with some great solutions, through networking and trial and error.

ROACHES (STURDY LITTLE DEVILS)

A cockroach can live nine days *without its head* before it starves to death. Sturdy little devils is an understatement! Cockroaches have been around for literally thousands of years, and chances are good they'll never show up on the endangered species list. These bugs have evolved into one of the most enduring pests you'll ever encounter. Researchers come up with great new products to eliminate them, and the roaches' response is to evolve their way out of it.

Cockroaches are prevalent throughout the United States. When our family lived in Florida, it was common practice to have your home sprayed on a monthly basis, to keep roaches from invading. My mom lives in Florida, and she (and everyone else down there, it seems) prefers to call them "Palmetto" bugs, after the tree of that name. In my opinion, a cockroach by any other name is still a cockroach. There are many varieties, and all of them give me the creeps. They're not welcome in my rentals, and I tend to associate their presence with dirty people, although this isn't always the case. In Florida, the Palmetto bugs are common pests, and many residents hire an exterminator to spray for them monthly.

It amuses me when one of my tenants calls to complain about "waterbugs" in the apartment. They usually tell me they've killed a couple of them and want me to take a look. Being the attentive landlord, I go to the apartment to check things out. One glance at the dead bodies tells me what I already know…a cockroach by any other name is still a cockroach. You can call them waterbugs if you like, but that doesn't change the facts. Actually, I've had a couple cases that really did involve waterbugs, and there's a quick remedy for them. A company called Prescription Treatment makes a product, CY-Kick CS™ that will take care of the problem. It's a liquid that, when diluted and sprayed in the area, usually the basement, will kill the bugs and repel them for months. It also helps repel spiders and other creepy crawlers.

But, back to the roach issue…How and why do they invite themselves into peoples' homes? Here in the Midwest, I've found that when tenants don't keep their apartments clean, roaches set up camp throughout the entire house, including the neighboring apartment. The only major infestations I've had have come with filthy tenants. Coincidence? I think not.

There have been times, however, when a perfectly neat and clean family calls to inform me they've seen a couple roaches. In these cases, the roaches or their eggs have been brought into the house in a paper grocery bag, or maybe a cardboard box that was used when the tenant moved into the apartment. The tenant may not even realize this has happened, because roaches tend to dislike daylight and/or light from lamps and ceiling fixtures. They stay hidden, often under sinks in kitchens and baths (they like damp areas), under appliances, and in cabinets and drawers. If the tenant isn't very observant, he/she may not notice the problem until it's become a serious infestation. How do you know if there's an infestation? You know it's *really* bad when there are roaches on the floors or walls in the middle of the day. If they're out crawling around, they're foraging for food; they haven't been able to find enough to eat in the dark, because they're competing with hundreds of others for the food.

A few years ago, with the intention of adding a couple more rentals to my portfolio, I had my realtor show me several properties. One of them had a severe roach problem. When I walked in, the tenant was sprawled across a dirty sofa, watching TV. Although I was looking at Ralph as I introduced myself, my peripheral vision revealed numerous roaches scurrying across the floor and walls. Were they invisible to him, or what? He was totally comfortable in their midst. The mere presence of roaches isn't enough to put me off, but the property had serious foundation issues as well, so I didn't buy it. Through the years, I've had to deal with cockroach infestations in my properties, and it never ceases to amaze me when the tenants don't seem to mind sharing the apartment with these pests.

So, what's the best method of getting rid of the cockroaches? Initially, I did what my tenants, friends and business associates advised me to do. I went to my local home improvement store and bought several bombs to place in the apartment. These are small cans that you open, put one in every room, and press a tab to release the spray into the room. You must leave immediately, because the fumes are toxic, and it's recommended you stay away for several hours. Upon your return, there should be hundreds of bodies that were stopped dead in their tracks. Unfortunately, these are minimally effective.

Shortly following my personal roach bomb story, I passed a pest control business that had a sign in the window, advertising their willingness to sell to the public. I did a U-turn and checked it out. Minutes later, I walked out with three syringes of Max Force™, which is a bait gel made by Bayer AG (1-800-331-2867). This is a truly amazing product, and I've been using it for several years. It's very easy to use; you apply a thin line of the gel along the inside edge of a cabinet, or behind the stove or refrigerator, or along the baseboard, wherever you've seen roach activity. I've actually watched them come right up to the gel and sample it. They love the taste, they invite their friends and family to the free buffet behind the stove, and when I return the next day, the kitchen floor is a mass grave. It's a beautiful thing. Bad infestations have been totally wiped out in a matter of days with this stuff.

Hopefully, you'll locate a pest control company that's willing to sell directly to you; if this isn't a common practice of theirs, perhaps you can persuade them by saying you have lots of rentals and that you'll use their services/products for every extermination need. Buying all my extermination weapons from this company has saved me hundreds of dollars over the years.

MICE AND RATS

As portrayed in the cartoons, mice have cute little faces, bright twinkling eyes, and graceful little whiskers that twitch when they sniff at a piece of cheese. In reality, people don't see them as benign or harmless, and many are scared to death of them. Although I don't fall into this category, I don't appreciate it when mice or rats gain access to one of my rentals. Little field mice love to come inside when the weather gets cool, and I have a problem with them from time to time. But I've only had one encounter with rats.

I'd bought a two-story house with a basement, and it had been empty for over a year. If you'll remember, it was the house where the squatters had filled the toilet with goodies. Well, those squatters weren't the only inhabitants. They shared the property with a colony of rats. The basement was unfinished, and housed the furnace and water heater. When I looked at the place, I had to use my flashlight because there was no electricity. Upon descending the rickety steps to the basement, I detected lots of movement to my right and left. Although my light never zeroed in on one, I'm sure the sounds belonged to the rats I'd startled upon entering. After quickly checking the furnace and water heater, I got out of there.

Before taking possession of the house, I bought several big rat traps. Armed with a jar of peanut butter that I kept in my car, I loaded the traps immediately after closing on the house. The following morning, I unloaded the traps. Every day for a couple weeks, I loaded and unloaded...babies, teenagers, etc., right down to the grandmas and grandpas! The numbers started to dwindle after that, and within three weeks, I wasn't seeing any more rats. This rat story is extreme, and most of the time, you'll only deal with mice.

If you live in cool weather, mice will find their way into your rental. I've tried to plug every hole in every foundation and basement, but somehow they manage to find a little crevice somewhere. My friend Carrie, who pitches in when she has extra time, always asks about mice before she agrees to come help paint an apartment. She's truly afraid of them, and doesn't want any confrontations. On a recent occasion, paintbrush in hand, she ventured into the dining room to trim around the windows. I was in the next room, cleaning. A terrified shriek made me drop what I was doing and run to her aid. There she was, arms flailing while her legs pumped up and down in an exaggerated marching/hopping motion...the "mouse dance." She'd seen a mouse scurry across the room and disappear into the heat vent. Unfortunately, her paintbrush was loaded with off-white paint when she started the dance; the brush had flown out of her hand and was resting on the *dark green* carpet in a pool of paint. A heavy spray of it also adorned the window, the wall and a few places on the carpet.

Even if you don't see any mice, you may come across their droppings. You may treat the house with Final Block™, which is a poison pellet that can be placed behind stoves and refrigerators, in basements, and yes, dropped into heat vents. I bought it from my trusty pest control people, who told me it's much more effective than anything you can buy elsewhere. Final Block is manufactured by Bell Laboratories, and can be used commercially, as in offices, warehouses, semi trailers, and even sewers. You'll sometimes see evidence of mice around baseboards and floors, where they've chewed a hole; I used to block the hole with steel wool, which mice will not chew up. As an experiment, I placed a pellet of Final Block at the entrance of one of these holes. The next day, it was gone; they'd dragged it off to their nest. Perfect! As with many pest control products, Final Block shouldn't be handled or eaten by pets or children.

TERMITES

I've had a couple run-ins with termites over the past ten years. In both cases, I was alerted to the problem when I noticed a section of flooring was soft. Upon closer inspection, which involved peeling back a piece of the sheet vinyl, I discovered the termites, who were busy eating up the wood underlayment and the joists beneath it. A trip to the basement revealed an industrious little colony that was demolishing about three feet of a joist.

Termites are easily recognized. They look like ants with wings, and part of their body is whitish in color. Surrounding them will be tunnels they've created in the wood as they've eaten away at it. I don't mess with termites; I call my pest control company instead of trying a do-it-yourself remedy. In both instances where termites had invaded, the company used Sentricon™, which is a bait system. At six- to eight-foot intervals around the perimeter of the house, they insert a container with a nice, fresh piece of pine inside. The pine has been treated with poison, which the termites ingest. They never reach the house itself, and if you've fixed the damage they caused in the first place, you should be home free. I have a yearly contract, whereby the pest control people come check the bait containers every couple months to see if there's been termite activity. There hasn't been a recurrence, but I'd rather be safe than sorry. The periodic checks represent peace of mind for me as the homeowner.

I'd recommend taking a good look at the floor joists when you're in the basement, and beware of any floor that has a soft spot. If you suspect termite activity, have an inspection performed by a reputable pest control company.

DOGS AND CATS

Being an animal lover myself, it was difficult initially to enforce the no pets clause contained in my lease. But what I eventually learned (the hard way, of course) was that many tenants have a hard enough time taking care of themselves, let alone having the added responsibility of a pet on the premises.

Dogs and/or cats:

1) Chew and scratch. I've had dogs try to dig holes in the carpet, resulting in huge areas where it's frayed and threadbare. Cats' claws can also damage carpet. When a dog's motivated to get in or out, it'll tear up the door and trim as it tries to scratch or chew its way in or out.

2) Make annoying noises. There's nothing worse than a dog barking when you're trying to get some sleep, especially when the barking is coming from the neighbor's apartment right next door. Cats, too, can make some pretty awful, annoying sounds. Tenants have tried countless times to sneak cats and dogs into their apartments; when I confront them, they usually tell me they're keeping it for a friend, to which I respond, "Tell your friend if it's not out by tomorrow, I'll have to file eviction."

3) Use the apartment as a toilet. Before I got into the habit of doing periodic checks on my interiors, I had some really nasty situations arise due to owners neglecting the pets they'd sneaked into their apartments. In one instance, a cat had had kittens, and *all* of them were using the entire house as a litter box. In another, the evicted tenants left behind a scrawny mutt. There was dog poop everywhere, which the tenants had stepped in, embedding it into the carpet.

4) Bring fleas into the apartment. *More* uninvited guests!

The worst outcome for having pets in the apartment is the cat urine problem. The smell is worse than dog urine, and more difficult to eradicate. If the cat has only used the carpet as a litter box once or twice, there's a chance you can take care of the smell. But if there are no visible stains, how do you locate the urine spots? A simple way to do this is with a black light. Nature's Miracle makes one (I got mine through a catalog), and I've also seen them in the large pet store chains. Actually, a black light is a black light…a leftover from the disco era will do the trick as well. The urine spot will glow like a white T-shirt under the black light. Finding the spot is the first challenge. The second and more difficult one is to get rid of the odor wafting up from the spot. If there's an obvious stain, I use my trusty Krud Kutter on it. But the odor is another issue altogether. Many assume that spraying the area with a deodorizing spray will take care of it, but this isn't true. If you don't get that odor out and your next tenant tries to sneak a cat in, the cat will go right to that spot and urinate there. There are products available at pet supply stores that have been developed to eliminate urine odors from carpets. They're enzyme-based, and will break up the protein in the urine; a normal cleaning product won't do the trick. Follow the instructions on the container, and make sure you soak the carpet all the way through with the solution! Any urine still present in the carpet or pad will bring back that odor.

One of the rentals I purchased had been inhabited by a ferret, or according to the stench, a family of ferrets. There were little piles of feces in every corner, and the entire place reeked so badly it made my nose and eyes burn. The ferret situation enabled me to buy that house cheaply; I'll bet no one else could get past the front door. I simply ripped out all the carpet, mopped the sub-flooring with watered down bleach, and started the fix up process.

As I mentioned earlier, there are always exceptions to the no pets rule, and I've made exceptions from time to time. I never allow tenants to bring a pet with them upon moving in, unless they're willing to show me the condition of the home they and their pet are currently occupying. Without this kind of information, it's too early to know what kind of tenant they're going to be. I've relented later on, though, as in the case of Judy, who'd been with me for a year. Mice were always invading her apartment, and she begged for a cat. I agreed, and the mouse problem disappeared, only to be replaced by the flea problem! I forgot to talk to her about keeping the cat indoors.

If you allow tenants to keep pets in their apartments, you may be dealing with fleas at some point. As with roaches, there are bombs you can buy and set off in the apartment. They don't work any better than the roach bombs. They may kill several fleas, but not all the fleas, and your problem will persist. A smarter alternative is a product called Ultracide™, which is made by Prescription Treatment and can be bought at your pest control company. It comes in a spray can, and you treat all the infested areas, including beds or furniture. Ultracide will kill all the adult fleas, and prevent re-infestation for seven months. Although they maintain that hatched pupal cases will not survive, I usually retreat after two weeks, just for insurance.

I've gone into apartments and not realized fleas were present. Particularly if you're wearing long pants, you may not notice the fleas. On one occasion, I cleaned the apartment and touched up paint everywhere (including along all the baseboards), and didn't know there were fleas in there until I got home, took off my pants, and noticed twenty or thirty bites surrounding my ankles and calves. I'd been so busy at the apartment, I didn't feel them biting me. Although I quickly threw all my clothes in the washer and dumped my shoes in the garage, it was too late. Now my house had fleas! (Dumbass attack # 973.)

This incident taught me what I should've known already...it's wise to take off your clothes and shoes before you go into your own home. If you don't have a garage, change clothes before you leave the hood.

DEAD BODIES, ETC.

Occasionally, I encounter some pretty nasty odor situations. Rodents die in crawl spaces or behind a wall, out of reach. The stench that emanates from a dead animal is unmistakable and very pungent. Fortunately, I've discovered a product that will take care of it. It's called Fresh Wave™ and can be found by going to www.fresh-wave.com. It comes in many forms, including candles, spray, and Super Gel crystals, which is what I use. The Super Gel can be bought in a 64-oz. container for about $50. Fresh Wave is worth every penny; a small amount of product goes a long way.

When I encounter a dead animal odor and can't locate the carcass to remove it, I put a few tablespoons of Fresh Wave in the area of the smell. Eventually, the odor from a dead animal just goes away, but until that time, Fresh Wave will absorb the odor and eliminate it.

I recently had a family of cats take up residence in one of my crawl spaces. They had used the entire crawl as a litter box, among other things. The entire house smelled awful. Once I discovered how they'd gotten in (one of the foundation blocks was loose) I formulated a plan. I hooked up a garden hose to the outdoor spigot near the normal access to the crawl space, and shot a hard spray of water into the crawl. The cats (who hate water) panicked and ran out the other exit. Once they had vacated their kitty condo, I moved the foundation block back into place. The cats were gone for good, but they left me that terrible smell as a souvenir. I threw a few spoonfuls of super gel into the crawl space, and also sprinkled some down the heat vents in every room of the house above. Voila! The house smells wonderful now. This product has a minty eucalyptus fragrance that isn't overpowering, and it is non-toxic, safe for people and pets.

Whether you're dealing with dead bodies, pet odors, musty basements, mildew, grease, or even skunk fumes, Fresh Wave will give you relief.

OTHERS (INCLUDING THE TWO-LEGGED VARIETY)

The biggest shock I've had, pet-wise, concerned an apartment that was rented by a family of five who turned out to be pests themselves. Every time I stopped by, the family seemed to have grown by one or two kids or adults. When questioned, the tenant assured me these were relatives that were visiting for a couple days. Maybe that was true; there's no way to know the truth in this situation. When I filed eviction on them for non-payment, I offered them the usual bribe.

"If you're out by Sunday night and leave the place clean and empty, we won't pursue you through the court system."

Dangling the carrot worked, but only partially. Yes, they left. But the only stuff they took was the clothes on their backs and some kitchen items. There were old tattered couches, some dingy, sticky end tables, and tons of junk left behind. (Cleanup in aisle 3…) If that were all I had to deal with, things would've gone smoothly. However, they also left behind a veritable *zoo*. Mind you, this happened early on in my career, before I instituted the apartment check routine. Two mangy mutts, a mother cat and six or seven kittens, two large snakes (caged, thank God), one parakeet and two other large exotic birds had been abandoned along with the apartment. How had they gotten away with this? Actually, it wasn't very difficult. When I stopped at that apartment, I never ventured beyond the first room inside the door. Another hard lesson learned.

So, what became of the zoo? I was able to find homes for all three birds, and the snakes. I thought calling Animal Control was the solution to the rest of the problem. However, the cats kept running behind and under furniture, and the mutts were the only animals they could corral. So, I had to move everything out of the apartment, and call Animal Control again. Their second trip to the apartment proved successful, and I was able to begin the process of getting the apartment back to par.

Worse, even, than the neglected pet problem is the "terrible tenant" infestation. It's incredible how much damage and filth can be left behind by these people. They're smarter than dogs and snakes; shouldn't they know better? The terrible tenant needs to be warned once, and then exterminated (i.e. evicted). Fortunately, expanding on my lease over the years has made it much easier to get rid of terrible tenants.

THE BOTTOM LINE

I'm an animal lover, but I've learned to say no to them in my rentals. Unless you have an established relationship with a quality tenant, it's risky business when you allow a total stranger to bring in a pet. In a very short time, that pet can become a pest.

The most common pests, roaches and mice, can be taken care of without involving an exterminator. Find a company that'll sell you the products over the counter, and do it yourself.

Although tenants don't always inform you about pest infestations, most of these will be noticed in your apartment checks. Keeping an eye on the apartments and their inhabitants is essential; if you're too busy with other things, or too lazy to remain vigilant about upkeep, you'll pay for it in the end. Remember this…your apartment checks are the key to exterminating every pest detailed in this chapter!

CHAPTER ELEVEN
ACCOUNTING (EENIE, MEENIE, MINEY, MO)

HERE WE GO...MORE MATH and numbers! The concept of accounting and record keeping can be somewhat intimidating for the beginner investor. Actually, if you do a decent job of organizing your records, receipts, etc., your accountant will take it from there. First of all, I highly recommend finding an experienced tax advisor who's familiar with the ins and outs of real estate investing. You can go with a tax preparer, an accountant or a CPA (Volkswagen to Cadillac, in that order). You may find one through other investors, or even through your realtor.

I happened to have a friend who's a CPA and I asked her to help me out. If you use an expert, you don't have to worry about becoming one yourself. CPAs are required to stay up to date on yearly changes in tax laws that affect real estate investors, and although it may cost more money to use a CPA, in most cases the fees are tax deductible. Rana has saved me thousands of dollars with her expertise through the years. Aside from the yearly consultation prior to filing my return, I haven't needed more than an occasional phone call with her to answer additional questions. Numerous tax advantages complement this type of work. I won't go into them here, because I don't really know how it all works. But Rana does; the deductions, depreciation, and other tax breaks allow me to stay in a lower tax bracket while maximizing my income.

Many investors think in terms of after-tax costs and after-tax income. I don't. For example, if you're in the 28% tax bracket, 28 cents of every dollar you *earn* goes to taxes (sigh…) but on the other hand, 28 cents out of every dollar you *spend* toward your rental is deductible. If you buy a $50 item for one of your rentals, that item only costs you $36. (28% of $50 is $14. You get to deduct $14 from the $50, giving you the after-tax cost of $36 for the item.) On the other hand, when someone gives you $600 for rent, 28% ($168) goes to taxes. Fortunately, when you calculate all the deductions, depreciation, interest and other tax advantages given to investors, we can often show a loss for the year even though we've had a very positive cash flow. It's a beautiful thing! Although I don't think in terms of after-tax costs and after-tax income, I'm fortunate to have a veteran CPA who does. Finding someone who'll make the most of the tax breaks available to you is of utmost importance. Spending a little more money in this area is a good idea.

Before buying my first property, I sat down with Rana and talked to her about setting up my business. I'd compiled a lengthy list of questions, and left her office with a pretty good idea of what was needed. She knew I wanted to keep things simple, and several years down the road, I'm *still* keeping it simple. Accounting issues don't ruffle my feathers. Learning a little bit about the accounting segment of the business has enabled me to do a better job of recording the necessary items for tax purposes. Hopefully, the information I share in this chapter will help you be well-organized and methodical, thus eliminating much of the hassle associated with accounting and tax reporting.

SETTING IT UP

The first item on my list of questions was, "What is the easiest, cheapest way to set up my business? Do I have to create an LLC (Limited Liability Company) in order to proceed?" I had been told by other investors that an LLC would be a good choice but I wasn't thrilled about the option, because:

1) I knew it would cost $1,000-$2000 to set it up through an attorney.
2) The tax reporting chores would be very detailed and time-consuming.

Money was very tight for me, and I was hoping to keep the paperwork and costs to a minimum. Against the better judgment of those advising me, I chose to do business as a Sole Proprietorship, which may sound fancy, but it's not at all. I picked a company name (my maiden name), had business cards made, which included the company name, my name underneath (no title), no address, and my contact information. No trips to the attorney, no trips to the City/County Offices, and no outlay of money…this was definitely the easiest way to go. My Sole Proprietorship worked well for me over the years. The advantages, as I mentioned, are the cost (nothing) and simplicity of setting it up. The record keeping is very easy as well.

However, there are two major disadvantages to the Sole Proprietorship option. One is that people can find out, through public records, that you're the official owner of the property. I've only had this happen once. Secondly, if a lawsuit is filed against you, the Sole Proprietorship doesn't protect your personal assets. Liability-wise, you must protect yourself by obtaining an umbrella insurance policy attached to your homeowner's insurance. If you're married or think you might be at some point, talk to your tax advisor about the Sole Proprietorship option. It can be a complicated issue when there's a spouse involved, if you want to keep the investment property as a separately held asset.

Rana suggested I open a separate account for my business, making it easier to keep my business and personal expenses separate. This is very important; when tax time rolls around, everything has to be filed separately. You don't want to commingle your personal spending with your business spending. Your business account checks have the company name, with your name and contact information underneath.

The most popular type of ownership company is the LLC (Limited Liability Company). Although it's costly, the LLC offers liability protection for its members, anonymity, and tax advantages too. Although there are single member LLCs, you may also run your business as an LLC if you have a partner with whom you've decided to work. If things don't work out or situations change, the LLC insures a valuation and 50-50 split of everything. I know that some people take on a partner for financial reasons but if it were me, I'd much rather take a personal loan from that person than give him/her a piece of the action. Most investors prefer the LLC to other partnerships and corporations. Talk to your advisor about the pros and cons of ownership options; he/she can help choose one to fit your situation.

By the way, today's technology allows you to have several of your rental bills, mortgages, and utilities paid by automatic withdrawal from your business account. Again, this saves time and effort. Contact the business office to get it set up. You may also have rent transferred from your tenant's account directly into your business account. Your bank can provide you with the appropriate form, which your tenant will fill out along with a voided check from his/her account. You and your tenant can plan for the EFT (electronic funds transfer) to occur on the day rent is due. The transaction may take a couple days to complete, but it simplifies the rent-collecting chore.

In addition to the separate bank account and business cards, I acquired a business-only credit card. Later, I authorized Craig as a second signer, and had the company send me a second card for him. This may seem foolish, but with a trusted associate like Craig, it works. He keeps all receipts, marks them with the address of the property concerned, and hands them over to me on a regular basis. The home improvement stores acknowledge him as an authorized cardholder on that account, and the arrangement has saved me countless trips to pick up supplies.

I haven't mentioned much about real estate attorneys. Because I was a Sole Proprietor, I didn't require an attorney's help in setting up my business. However, I've had questions and needed advice throughout my career, and I'm fortunate to have a savvy real estate attorney available to me. I found him through other investors. Don't assume all your written forms are complete and within the letter of the state and local statutes. Take them to a real estate attorney and have him/her look them over. And while you're at it, compile a good list of any other questions you might have. I've only had to sit down with my attorney a few times over the years, but it's comforting to know he's only a phone call away.

Having chosen a company name, ordered business cards and checks, I was ready to set up shop as an official business entity. It was time to gather the materials I'd need for record keeping.

CONFESSIONS OF A 70S GIRL

Okay, so this is just a little embarrassing but until I began writing this book, I didn't own a computer. When I started my business, I didn't have the money or time to invest in a computer. So I bought a thirteen-column ledger book and organized my business on paper. But whether you have your rentals on paper or in the computer, the record keeping chores will be the same. The manner in which you enter them is the only difference.

For the past several years, I've done quite well with my little antiquated system, but when the decision was made to write this book, my eighty-one-year-old mom and my daughter Allison *shamed* me into having my mom send me her old laptop. As Allison jokingly said,

"C'mon, Mom, take the leap! Jump into the twenty-first century. Trust me, it won't kill you!"

I recently moved my business information to the computer, onto Microsoft Excel spreadsheets. I'll address various computer programs later in the chapter. I'm kicking myself for not doing this spreadsheet thing years ago. The columns total themselves, and I've saved myself so much time! I transfer everything to a flash drive when I file my month-end receipts, just in case my computer crashes. But whether your business is recorded on paper or entered into a computer, there are specific requirements as to what's reported, for tax purposes.

From the start, organizational skills have been a strong point for me. I was motivated to keep track of how well my properties were performing. With good record keeping, you'll know if you're making a good profit or losing your shirt. I've never been audited and the thought doesn't particularly scare me, except for the incredible hassle involved, because I trust my books and my CPA. But if record keeping isn't your thing and you get audited, you'll have big problems with "the big boys." So, if you get a few months into this journey and find you're slacking in the record keeping area, you'd best hand those responsibilities off to someone who will take care of the details for you.

RECEIPTS, ETC.

The good news is, you'll probably start out with only one or two properties, which is very manageable. Keeping track of receipts is your most important record keeping chore. Canceled checks or credit card statements aren't sufficient, although they should be retained, too.

Especially throughout the fix-up process, you're going to accumulate piles and piles of receipts. I usually stuff them in my purse and deal with them later, but you may want to keep a folder or other container in your car specifically to hold the receipts you collect throughout your work day. I write the address of the property on the receipt at the time of purchase. With your first rental this isn't necessary, but when you have a bunch of rentals and stacks of receipts, it's helpful to have each one labeled. If you've bought things for three or four properties on one receipt, just make copies so they can be filed with the appropriate property. A couple times during the week, I dig the receipts out of my purse and put them in an empty drawer in my desk, where they stay until the end of the month when I do my filing. My CPA has rental property clients who come to her at year-end with a huge box of receipts that haven't been sorted or filed. It takes hours for her to sort and assign these receipts to the appropriate properties, so that she can start working on the tax return. A little attention to detail at the end of each month could've saved these investors hundreds of dollars in CPA fees. Filing your receipts monthly eliminates stress and panic at tax time.

One of the more annoying record keeping duties you'll have is tracking the work-related mileage on your car. You'll get deduction per mile on your tax return, and it really mounts up. When I began my real estate investing career, I didn't have a separate car devoted to work. Now I do, which makes tracking mileage easier. You'll need to buy a small notebook in which to record your daily work-related miles driven. Work miles includes anything involving your rental business: driving to the bank to make deposits, trips to the home improvement store, checking out potential homes to buy, visiting mortgage brokers or other business people, going to court, anything related to your rentals. On each entry, you need the date, number of miles driven, and where/ why you went. Annoying? Most definitely. I hate taking the time to do this, but if I were audited, the IRS would want me to produce a mileage notebook. I have a friend who takes his laptop with him daily and records his work miles on the computer; I guess that might hold up okay with the IRS, but my dog-eared notebook looks a heck of a lot more authentic.

At the end of every month, get out your calculator, pencil and columnar pad, if you're recording everything on a paper ledger. Add up all the receipts you've accumulated over the month. Regardless of whether it's on paper or in the computer, it's important to file your receipts monthly. For tax reporting, receipts will be filed under three general areas: a specific rental property, the business name, or your personal dwelling. Wherever possible, attach each receipt to a specific property. For example, if I put an ad in the paper for two of my properties, instead of filing the $40 bill under my business name, I'll split it 50/50 and file it under each property address. The only receipts that should be filed under your general business name are things like paint, tools, cleaning supplies, legal and other advice, signage, postage/printing, education, or anything else that just can't be assigned to a specific property.

If you work out of your home like I do, you can get extra deductions because you have a home office. So you'll need to keep all records of utility bills, maintenance, etc. for your home so your tax advisor can use this information to save you money at tax time.

If the bulk of your income is through rental properties, you'll file taxes quarterly. The amounts are estimated, based on last year's tax returns. In this business, due to changes in tax law and changes in your business, your quarterly payments can change quite a bit. Fortunately, you and your tax advisor can predict the changes and prepare for them in advance.

For each of my properties, I label the top of the ledger sheet (or spreadsheet) with the property address, parcel number (legal description), the date of purchase and how much I paid for it. The months go across the top of the page horizontally, and these categories go down the left edge of the page, vertically:

- Rent
- Electricity
- Gas
- Water
- Repairs

- Supplies
- Advertising
- Evictions
- Property Taxes
- Property Insurance
- Capital Improvements (These long-lasting improvements, such as roofs, furnaces, siding, water heaters, porches, etc. are depreciated over several years instead of deducted in a single year on your tax return, so they must be kept separate for accounting purposes. A capital improvement, as opposed to a normal repair, makes the property more valuable, long-lived or more useful than it was before the improvement.)

All the receipts I gather throughout the month will fall into one of the above categories. Under my general business name, I use the following categories:

- Cell Phone
- Supplies
- Advertising
- Printing/Postage
- Repairs
- Business Meals
- Capital Improvements
- Education
- Gifts
- Management Income
- Other Income (Consulting, etc.)
- Other Expense

Whether you record your rental information in a paper ledger or type them into a computer, this is a tedious, time-consuming endeavor, particularly if you own several properties. But it's a very important one. At year-end, the 13th column provides the total for the year. Doing this by hand takes time; the computer will keep running totals automatically. The totals aren't just important from a tax reporting standpoint, they're also important because *they tell you how your rental's performing.* So if you're like me and this stuff bores the hell out of you, suck it up and get over it!

After I've recorded the receipts for each property at the end of the month, I staple them together and put them in the appropriate folder in my filing cabinet. Each property has its own folder, separate from its ownership file which I keep elsewhere in a fireproof filing cabinet. And really, that's about it. At year-end, I take the receipts out of the folders, put them all together in a huge expandable brown envelope, and store them away. Prior to April 15th, I meet with Rana, totaled ledger sheets in hand. I save all records and tax returns for seven years. Check with your tax advisor to find out how long you should keep yours.

TAKING CARE OF (OTHER PEOPLE'S) BUSINESS

After I'd been taking care of my own rentals for a few years and had become confident in all facets of the business, including the record keeping, I agreed to do property management for another real estate investor. I've not chosen to give my own management responsibilities to someone else, because:

- I believe I'll fill my vacancies faster and smarter than someone else will
- I like having control over my tenant selection
- Managing my properties keeps me involved and aware of the condition of the properties
- I like keeping *all* the income rather than giving a percentage to a management company

There are tons of people out there who love the tax advantages of owning investment properties but would rather jump off a cliff than manage them on their own. That's where I (you?) come in. When I was approached regarding property management, the situation seemed ideal:

1) The investor only had one property. I could get my feet wet without totally diving in.

145

2) The property was near a university, which meant it would generate a high rental income, i.e. high percent management fee for me.

These factors prompted me to take interest in the job, and I started searching for a management contract I liked. As usual, I ended up with a combination of several I'd seen. I did a little sleuth work by calling a few property management companies in the area to find out how they operated and what kind of fees they charged. Because I feel it's advantageous to have only one person handling everything, and because I make myself available 24/7, I thought I could charge a little more than the others (12% rather than 10%). My owners were impressed with what I offered and we've had a wonderful working relationship for several years. They've acquired additional property that I also manage.

My property management income qualifies as ordinary income and is taxed accordingly, so it's reported separately from my rentals. I have a category called "other income" under which I record these monies. When I took on the property management responsibilities, I also decided to take on labor such as painting, small repair work, etc. for those clients, at my own discretion. If I weren't busy at the time, maybe I'd do work at their rental when we had a turn-around, and charge them a reasonable rate for my time. So I included that option in my contract.

When someone calls me regarding property management, I send him or her a letter of introduction like the one I'm including here. It's a good idea to write out something like this, as a way of marketing yourself to potential clients. I'm also including a copy of the contract and lease agreement I've used. Although it's longer than the one I use for my own properties, I've condensed it as much as possible, making it short and easy to read.

INTRODUCTORY LETTER

Dear Mr. and Mrs. Green,

Thank you for your inquiry about my property management business. By way of introduction, I'd like to tell you a little about myself.

(You might give a brief background here.....age, educational background, career stats, family info, or whatever you feel pertinent. You want to create a positive image of you as a person, and your abilities as a manager.)

I've been purchasing single and multi-family rental homes for many years now. I fix them up and rent them out; I currently have 29 units.

When I began doing property management several years ago, my goal was to give my homeowners total peace of mind, so they'd not have to worry about their properties. I've had great success with this goal. If you'd like to speak with some of my clients, I'd be happy to provide references. My honesty and integrity have earned the trust and respect of all my clients.

As a "one-person-show" I can offer my homeowners much more than the large management companies can:

- I'm available 24 hours/day on my cell phone.
- I use (wherever possible) my own contractors who charge me less than the big companies do.
- After move-outs, I do as much of the work (cleaning, trash removal, carpet shampooing, minor repairs, painting, etc.) as possible, and charge only _____/hour for my time. The normal rates are _____/hour.
- Although I charge 12% of rents as my management fee, I don't take any of the deposit for myself. The large companies may only charge 10%, but will take 33% (and up) of the deposit for themselves.
- It's comforting for owners to know that I'm their only contact person, for whatever question or problem they might have. Often with larger companies, there's no continuity with their personnel.

You're never sure whom you're going to be dealing with when you need to resolve an issue.

I'm passionate about what I do and have become very skilled in all facets of my business over the years of its existence.

I've enclosed a copy of my management contract with this letter. Please feel free to call me if you have any questions or would like me to supply you with references.

Thanks again for your interest in my work…I look forward to hearing from you!

Best regards,

Barb Getty

MANAGEMENT AGREEMENT

This agreement is between Barnes Properties and _____
regarding the property located at _____

As the managing agent, Barnes Properties agrees to:

1) Secure tenants: Advertise, show, take applications, check references and arrange for move-in of new tenant.

2) Collect move-in deposit and rental payments: Collect rent in a timely manner and begin eviction process if lease is violated. Any late fees on rent collected will be paid to Barnes Properties. Rent will be deposited into an escrow account (set up by the owner), to which Barnes Properties will have access.

3) Repairs: Barnes Properties will manage all repairs/renovations associated with the property and pay for such repairs out of the escrow account. In the event repair is needed while the property is occupied, the tenant will contact Barnes Properties, who will arrange for the work to be done.

4) Expenses: Barnes Properties will pay, from the escrow account, any utilities, property taxes, insurance, etc. as dictated by the owner.

5) Move-outs: Barnes Properties will change locks, arrange for repairs, cleaning, painting, trash removal, etc. in preparation for showing the property to prospective tenants.

6) Accounting: Barnes Properties will file receipts and record all income and expenses relating to the property and provide such to the owner upon request. At year-end, for tax purposes, a complete written accounting will be given to the owner.

7) Compensation: Barnes Properties will deduct 12% of gross rents per month as payment for performing the above-mentioned duties.

This contract may be terminated at any time by either party, upon thirty days' notice.

Special provisions _____

We agree to the terms and conditions of this management contract.

_____   _____
           Barnes Properties   Owner

Date_____

RENTAL AGREEMENT

This agreement is made on _____ between Barnes Properties (Landlord) and _____ (Tenant). The property, located at _____ , will be rented for one year, beginning_____and ending_____.

ACCEPTANCE Tenant agrees to accept home as is, having already inspected it.

RENT Tenant will pay_____per month in advance, on or before the first day of the month. A $50 late fee will be due if rent is not *postmarked* by 5:00 p.m. on the 5th day of the month. If rent is not paid in good funds, Tenant will pay a $25 service charge. Rent must be paid with a check or money order.

UTILITIES Tenant will pay all bills associated with the property when due. These must be in the Tenant's name prior to moving in.

USAGE Property is to be used only as a residence and shall not be occupied by more than____people. Tenant acknowledges receipt of____keys. Should Tenant get locked out and require Landlord's assistance in gaining access to house, Tenant must pay Landlord $30 upon arrival.

DEPOSIT Tenant agrees to pay Landlord a deposit of_____. If at any time the Tenant breaks the lease or defaults in any of the provisions of the lease, the deposit will be applied to the Landlord's actual damages resulting from the breach of the lease. Upon completion of the lease term, Landlord may withhold from the deposit only what is reasonably necessary to cover the following: damage to the property, cleaning costs, unpaid rent or utility bills. No part of the rent will be applied to the Tenant's last month's rent. Deposit monies owed to the Tenant will be returned within 7 days after Tenant has moved out completely.

ALTERATIONS Tenant will not change, decorate or alter property (inside or out) without first obtaining Landlord's permission.

SUBLEASING Tenant will not sublease property without Landlord's permission.

LIQUID-FILLED FURNITURE Tenant agrees not to keep any liquid-filled furniture on the premises without Landlord's permission.

PARKING Tenant may park in the garage, driveway or on the street, never on the grass. Tenant agrees not to make any vehicle repairs at the property that will take more than two days to complete.

REPAIRS Tenant will contact Landlord when any repair is needed, and Landlord will undertake repair as soon as possible. Tenants must pay 100% of any repair that is caused by them or their guests.

DRAINS Tenant will not allow food/grease down any drains that don't have garbage disposals. Human waste and toilet paper are the only things to be flushed down toilets.

YARD Tenant agrees to keep home (inside), yard and garbage areas clean, mow grass and shovel snow when needed.

MANAGER The Landlord managing the property for the owner is Barb Getty, with Barnes Properties. Her contact information is: address here. Her home phone is xxx-xxx-xxxx and her cell is xxx-xxx-xxxx.

ACCESS Tenant agrees to allow Landlord access to property to inspect or show, to make repairs or improvements. Except in an emergency, Landlord will give advance notice of any visit.

INSURANCE Owner has insurance on the building; this does not cover the Tenant's possessions.

LAWFUL USE There will be no illegal activities on the premises.

SERVICE OF PROCESS Every Tenant who signs this lease agrees to be the agent of the other Tenants, and is authorized and required to accept, on behalf of the other Tenants, service of summons or other legal notices relative to the tenancy.

NOISE Tenants agree to keep TV, music and other noise at a reasonable level so as not to bother neighbors.

CONSEQUENCES Violation of any part of this agreement will result in eviction. Landlord will recover attorney fees, court costs and any other expenses involved.

ACKNOWLEDGEMENT Tenants acknowledge they have read, understand, and agree to the provisions of this contract.

SPECIAL PROVISIONS_____

_____

TENANT: _____
LANDLORD: _____

This rental agreement works well in my jurisdiction. Before using this or any of my other forms, have them checked by your attorney to make sure they fit the legal parameters for your county.

If you decide to get into managing for other people, you might want to check on whether your state requires you to have a leasing license to do this work. I've heard the license is usually inexpensive and easy to obtain, so don't view this as a stumbling block.

I enjoy my property management business. The properties I manage draw high rents (I wouldn't have it any other way) so the income from management fees is decent. Because these management properties are high-end, the tenants:

1) Are on year leases
2) Pay all utilities
3) Almost always pay rent on time
4) Always call me if something's not working right
5) Are easy to manage

The $210/month I make on the $1400/month house I manage is easy money. I may go months in a row without a call from that house… no-stress money. I'm always happy to add more high-end management homes to my portfolio. Yes, there's work to be done when tenants move out, and occasionally you'll have problems throughout a tenancy, but managing higher-end properties is a nice addition to my rental income.

If you become an expert at managing your own properties, you might consider managing for other investors or private individuals. Depending on the property, this can be a low-stress source of income.

KEEPING IT ALL STRAIGHT

Whether you keep your records in a ledger or on a computer, it's essential that you keep it organized, one way or the other. As you add more properties, putting everything on the computer makes sense.

If you decide to computerize, I'd suggest the entry-level Quicken program for general business accounting. This program will streamline your accounting and is easy to use, but the downfall to it is you can't tailor it to your particular needs. If you want to do your own thing, you might try the electronic spreadsheet by Microsoft Excel, which is more flexible than the Quicken program. If you've been using ledger sheets to record your information, you can duplicate these on Excel, and the program will automatically add all the columns for you, throughout the year. If you're technologically advanced, you might try Quickbooks, which allows you to do all the above, plus many more functions such as check writing. Your personality and motivation will dictate your choice of accounting program. I'd suggest talking with other investors about what they use.

Sometimes, software sellers will allow you to try a program free of charge before purchasing it. Or if not, maybe they'd lend you an extra instruction booklet so that you could look it over before buying. Whichever way you go---paper or computer---make sure you stay current with your record keeping. Only a small percentage of people get audited, but if the IRS starts breathing down your neck, you'd best be prepared!

THE BOTTOM LINE

Although I find the whole accounting thing a total bore, I do appreciate the importance of detailed record keeping. First and foremost, find a tax preparer that's well-versed in real estate tax law. Even though they're a little more costly, I recommend going with a CPA. You may find one through other investors, or even your realtor. If you use an expert, you don't have to worry about becoming an expert yourself.

Whether you set up your business as a Sole Proprietorship, LLC or other corporation, it's essential to keep your personal and business spending separate. Set up a business account and don't commingle monies. Save and label all receipts. Each property should have a permanent file, in a fireproof cabinet, that contains all the paperwork from the purchase of the property, and also a working file into which you put each month's receipts.

Managing properties for other people can be a nice addition to your rental income. If you choose high-end properties to manage, they should be relatively trouble-free. You can choose to make some extra cash on labor fees when tenants move out and painting/cleaning chores need to be done.

It doesn't really matter whether you do your accounting on paper or on a computer. The only thing that matters is that *you do it*. Yes, it's boring. Yes, it's time-consuming if you have a bunch of properties. But if you blow it off and get audited down the road, you'll be oh, so sorry. So, be disciplined about it and do it correctly.

The best reward of keeping accurate records is knowing how well (or poorly) each of my properties is performing. At year-end, I take a good look at all of them to see if I have any slackers in the group. If I didn't have accurate income/expense figures, there'd be no way to determine which of my rentals had a bad year. Sometimes, a dip in profits can be explained and remedied by making a few minor changes. If not, it's time to change gears and consider exit strategies, which leads us to the next chapter...

CHAPTER TWELVE
CHANGING GEARS

THE REAL ESTATE INVESTING market is always in a state of flux. As an investor, you must track the success or failure of your investment properties and be flexible. When one of your properties doesn't perform well, try to figure out why. This is where great record keeping comes in handy. Did you make some major costly improvements there, like a new roof or siding? Did you replace a water heater or furnace, or install new flooring or fixtures? Expenditures like these will decrease your profit for the year but increase the value of the rental; there's no cause for alarm. Profits will also suffer due to vacancy. If lack of rental income was the main problem, I hope it wasn't because you allowed a nonpaying tenant to stay and suck you dry.

READY TO GET RID OF ONE?

Three situations prompt me to get rid of property.

1) The first is a desire to free up money. Early on, I'd buy a duplex, fix it up, make rental income for a year or more, and then sell it for a nice profit. Between the money I'd invested and the profit I'd made, I was able to buy two more properties. Sweet deal, huh?

2) The second reason I sell property is to get rid of debt. Depending on your real estate investing plan, you may want to pay down debt when you get the chance. I've sold a couple properties to pay off

mortgages I had on them. The sale paid off the mortgages with enough money left over to purchase another property or get rid of another mortgage elsewhere. My goal has been to own several of my properties free and clear. The above strategies have worked well for me, and you may want to consider them as part of your strategy as well. Every investor has his/her own investment goals and will tailor selling strategies to those goals.

3) Take heed, however, to the third situation that prompts me to sell a property. This situation needs to be addressed *regardless* of your investment goals. If you're attentive to your rentals, you'll be aware of subtle changes in the neighborhood. For instance, I noticed it getting harder and harder to find and keep good tenants at one of my properties. I'd get tenants in, but find myself evicting them quickly for nonpayment. Then, the apartment would stand empty while I tried to find another candidate. Profits were down. Vacancies were up. The surrounding streets were still okay, but my particular block was starting to look a little shabby. Various shady-looking people were hanging out at all hours, and according to the criminologist at the police department, crime had increased. The other houses on my block were looking a bit neglected. These observations indicate changes that shouldn't be ignored. I put the house on the market immediately and was relieved to get rid of it. Keep your finger on the pulse of your rental neighborhood. Sometimes changes occur over which you have no control, and if you see things changing for the worse, it's time to get out.

SELLING OUTRIGHT/FLIPPING PROPERTIES

Before you sell one of your properties, sit down with your tax advisor and figure out what the tax implications of the sale will be. If you've owned the property for several years, you will have taken advantage of depreciation expense each year. Even if your property has had a good cash flow, when you subtract the depreciation from the income earned, you may show a loss on paper. The tax benefits of taking depreciation are great, but when you sell, the depreciation you've taken will be added back in, or recaptured, and will affect the capital gains you end up paying. I'm no tax expert, but I understand the importance of running the numbers with your advisor before marketing a property, whether you're selling outright, flipping or doing an installment sale.

With the new lower capital gains tax rates, many investors are choosing to sell investment property outright. For people who are looking to slow down or get out of the business altogether, this is the easiest route. List the property with a realtor, sell it, and take the money and run. I've done this with a few homes and simply reinvested the money in another property. The only downside to listing your property with a realtor is the commission you'll pay, typically 3½% to your realtor and 3½% to the buyer's realtor. But this fee is offset by the comfort of knowing all the details will be taken care of as you move through the process of selling the property. If you have substantial equity in a property and decide it's worth keeping, you might consider just refinancing that home, which will free up more cash for you to buy additional property.

If you're trying to sell your property when the market's in a slump, as it was through 2009-10, find out if your loan, if you have one, is assumable. If potential buyers can take over your loan payments, the property will be more attractive to them. If the interest rate on your loan is lower than the current rate, that's another plus. You'll want to check with your bank, however, to see what happens in the event the buyer defaults on the assumed loan. Do they come after you for the balance? If the buyer's paid down the balance and you don't mind getting the property back, fine. In a default situation, most lenders won't pursue you if a year or two has passed since the sale. Check with your lender.

Prior to putting a property on the market, take a good hard look at it from the street. What's your first impression? Be objective. As a potential buyer, would you be attracted to the home? If not, you've got work to do before putting a sign in the yard. Maybe you need to add some landscaping, or a decorative pot of flowers on the porch. I like to use artificial ones…they don't need water and they don't need trimming. A wreath on the door also adds charm. You may want to wash the front windows and siding, or do a little painting. If your rental's empty, you might purchase some colorful throw rugs and towels for the kitchen and bathrooms, and a hanging plant (again, fake is good) here and there. Also, you'll need to make sure you provide doormats, so no one will track in mud or dirt on wet days. If you're incapable of making a non-biased assessment of the outside/inside prior to listing the property, maybe your realtor or someone else can help you. There's a whole new industry out there called "staging," whereby an individual gives input regarding what you can do to improve the curb appeal and inside desirability of your home for potential buyers. Amazingly, this can be accomplished with little money invested on your part. Many realtors have connections with stagers and could provide you with contact numbers.

Properties are more attractive to potential buyers if they're filled with tenants. The buyer would prefer not to be burdened with the extra work of finding tenants after buying the rental, and will appreciate being able to make rental income immediately. Of course, the house shows better if the tenants are neat, clean people. I had a duplex on the market that had a great tenant on one side and a slob on the other. Before every showing, I had to nag the slob about making sure the apartment was clutter-free and clean. Clutter, etc. has never stopped me from buying a rental, but some buyers will be intimidated by it and walk away.

If you sell a property with the idea of buying another to replace it, talk to your tax advisor or real estate attorney about a 1031 exchange. This strategy's a little complicated, but will enable you to avoid paying taxes on the profit from the sale of your property, as long as the replacement property is "of like kind." The monies from the sale are held by a third party and you must earmark a maximum of three potential replacement properties within 45 days of the closing on the property you sold. Within 180 days after the closing, one of those properties must be purchased, and you must apply all the escrowed monies to the purchase of that second property. In a competitive real estate market, this time frame may be challenging; if you can't get it done in 180 days, the tax hit is all yours.

Flipping properties is a strategy that got lots of attention in the early 2000's, when interest rates were low and the housing market everywhere was booming. Many investors jumped on this bandwagon. My brother-in-law bought several properties in high-end communities near Phoenix, at pre-construction prices. By the time the homes were actually built, the prices had skyrocketed and he was able to sell (flip) them at a very nice profit. The demand was sufficient, and he made good money doing this until the market flattened out. It's a gamble that pays off, *as long as the value of the home goes up and there's demand for the housing.* He got out of it before the real estate market plummeted.

Those who didn't got stuck with homes they thought they were going to flip. When no buyers showed up, they were forced to slash the price, or become unwilling landlords and rent the home, in an effort to recoup some of the cash they'd invested.

One of the big disadvantages to buying a home and selling it quickly is the short-term capital gain you pay on the profit. If you sell the property within one year of the day you purchased it, you'll pay capital gains equal to your current tax bracket. Tax-wise, if your tax bracket is above the 15% mark, it's smart to hold the property for more than a year before reselling it. If you do so, you'll take advantage of the current 15% capital gains tax. But check with your tax advisor. Tax laws are always changing.

I've flipped a few properties through the years, and have done it in a low-risk manner. First of all, I buy what investors call distressed property. Every home I've bought has needed work. As mentioned early in the book, this is how you make money going in. I've sold a few on them outright, and taken the profit to reinvest in additional property or pay down debt elsewhere. Second, I buy in a decent neighborhood, fix it up, and do an installment sale, which I'll discuss later in this chapter. If you buy, fix and sell outright, you can realize a quick profit in a short amount of time, but you'll need to factor in the tax hit when you're adding up the potential profit from the sale. This is a great way to generate quick cash. Another plus of flipping is that you can start and stop the process at will.

A final warning about the joys of flipping...it's sort of like the gambling stories you've heard from friends. People are always quick to tell you about their big winnings, but you never hear about how much they've lost at the poker table or slot machines. If you buy a property with the intention to fix it and sell it quickly:

1) Make sure you're realistic about what the repair costs will be.

2) Know what you can ask for the home when it's finished.

3) Don't forget to factor in the capital gains taxes you'll pay when you flip the property.

4) If you're already in a high tax bracket, your situation may be adversely affected by the extra income you generate by flipping properties, since it's taxed as ordinary income.

5) Have a backup plan. What if the house doesn't sell in a month, or six months or, worse yet, a year? In the current market, this could happen to you. If you have a mortgage, that payment comes due no matter what. Profits go down the drain as the house sits empty. Flipping properties isn't a guaranteed promise of income. If you don't find an interested buyer, you may need to rent it out to generate some return on the investment.

I like flipping properties from time to time as part of my investment strategy, but I'd never rely on flipping as my sole source of income. It's not a guaranteed way to make money. Buying and holding properties has allowed me to accumulate wealth over time and take advantage of market appreciation. The increase in housing values has always stayed ahead of inflation increases, and if you're smart about picking your target area, your wealth will grow along with your rental property portfolio.

LAND CONTRACTS/LEASE OPTIONS

Note: Because of unscrupulous practices on the part of some mortgage loan originators, who granted loans to unqualified buyers through 2007, the government is in the process of passing laws to protect this from happening again. If you sell a home through a land contract, you may be considered a mortgage loan originator, and laws are being passed that will require you to be licensed. Check with your real estate attorney before proceeding.

A few years ago, one of my favorite tenants approached me about buying a house. He lived in one of my duplexes; his family lived in the front apartment, and his sister and her family lived in the back. Julio had a great job doing drywall work, and he'd been an excellent, long-term tenant. He loved the duplex, and questioned me about the possibility of buying it from me. Through our conversation, I learned that Julio:

1) Had no bank accounts
2) Had no Social Security number
3) Had no credit cards
4) Was not a U.S. citizen
5) Had $7000 cash for a down payment (woohoo!)

I loved this family…they were clean people who took pride in their home, and had never been late with a rent payment. I had no idea how I could sell them my duplex. Julio would never qualify for a traditional mortgage. I told him I'd do some checking and get back with him.

After making a few phone calls to my veteran investor friends, I came up with a solution. I would sell him the home "on contract." Since Julio, I've done several land contracts, or installment sales. For me, it's a terrific way to get rid of the daily responsibilities associated with ownership of a rental. As Julio's family grew, he enclosed the front porch to create additional living space, as seen in the following pictures. Julio wouldn't have qualified for a traditional mortgage, but he's been an excellent buyer who has made timely payments and has improved the home as well.

A few years back, mortgages were easy to obtain. Thousands of first-time buyers, many of whom had less-than-stellar credit, were able to purchase homes using adjustable-rate mortgages. Unfortunately, when the payments went up after three or five years, many of these buyers couldn't handle the payments, and they defaulted on their loans. Foreclosures in this country are on the rise. This unfortunate circumstance represents tremendous opportunity for the smart investor. Many of these buyers are being forced back into rental situations, and although their credit is now a mess, their ability to pay a reasonable, fixed-rate mortgage remains intact. These former homeowners can become buyers again. Aha! This is where you and I come in. They can buy our homes on land contracts.

When I sell a home on contract, I'm acting as the mortgage company. The buyer gives me a down payment, I charge him a monthly principal and interest payment and print out a payment schedule which I give him at our closing. The buyer pays all bills associated with the property. I have the insurance and property tax bills sent to me, but I add an amount on to their monthly payment to cover the cost. Basically, I'm the lender, and I hold the mortgage to the property. So the beauty of it is this: monthly income with no work. (You gotta love it.) Doing installment sales creates a steady stream of income for me over a long period of time. I find this strategy safer and more attractive than flipping.

I'd recommend talking with your real state attorney and other investors who've done land contracts before jumping into this selling strategy. Also, you'll want to sit down with your CPA to determine the tax impact of selling one of your properties on contract. For example, if you sell a property you've owned for several years, you'll have taken a lot of depreciation on that property over the years. You must pay taxes on *all* the depreciation in the first year of your land contract. Like any other sale, it's smart to talk with your CPA about tax implications before you jump in. This is very important!

I'm including copies of the forms I use; get copies of the forms other investors use, and make an appointment with your real estate attorney to have him check the paperwork and give it his seal of approval. Your attorney will know the legal ins and outs of selling your properties on contract in your state; I wouldn't proceed without his input.

When you're thinking about selling one of your properties on contract, look at comparable homes in the area. Look at others like yours on the market right now, and find out the asking price on those homes. I like to price my contract homes a little below market value. After all, you're foregoing realtor commissions and earning a very nice interest rate (see below), so don't be greedy. Also, if your buyer chooses to refinance down the road, you want the house to appraise at or above your purchase price.

The tenants with whom I've done these contracts can't qualify right now for regular mortgages. Some will never qualify. Therefore, since I'm taking on added risk by lending to them, I charge higher interest. I could get a mortgage today for about 5%; my buyers pay me 10%. I know other investors who charge interest rates that are more than twice the going rate. After a period of three years, I allow my buyers to refinance. If they can qualify, refinancing will get them a lower interest rate and lower payments, which is great. As for me, I've made a big chunk of money in interest; I'll take the money and buy another property, or pay down debt elsewhere. If they're able to refinance before the three-year mark, I usually make an exception and allow them to do so.

The biggest challenge in setting up the land contract business was the finance stuff. I found a great website (http://yona.com/loan/) to help me figure out mortgage amounts. If you know the loan amount, the length of the loan in months and your interest rate, this site will pop up the entire payment schedule, which you can print out and give to your tenant. But I also wanted to know and compare different payment/interest/payoff amounts, and I'd need to use a financial calculator for that. The mere thought of it made my blood run cold. One of my guru friends told me which model to buy, and walked me through what I needed to know. He wrote down which keys I needed to press to solve various problems, and for you "finance-phobes" out there, I'm going to reproduce the list here. The calculator I bought is an hp 12c platinum financial calculator, and here's how to use it, *bare bones*:

Let's say you're selling a house for $55,000 and your buyer has given you $5000 as a down payment. The loan amount is $50,000, and he'd like to own the house in 15 years. What will his payment be? The face of the hp 12c intimidates the hell out of me, but you don't have to press many keys to get your answers. Here they are:

1) f, then CLX will clear everything off the screen
2) 50000, then CHS, then PV (present value)
3) 15, then g, then n (15 year loan)
4) 10, then g, then i (10% interest)
5) PMT (payment)

The answer comes up as 537.30, which I round down to $537. The monthly taxes and insurance add up to $175/month, for a total of $712. Unfortunately, my tenant tells me he can't afford more than $650/month total, so I have to get the mortgage payment down to $475 ($650 − 175 = 475). With that 537.30 number still showing on your screen, you just punch in your new payment:

475, then PMT, then n

The number showing will be 253, which is the number of months it will now take to pay off the loan at the new, lower payment. Now, instead of 15 years, it will take them

253 months divided by 12 = 21.08 years.

For the purpose of making things easy on my buyer, I always figure the monthly payment as a round figure, like 650 or 800 instead of 637 or 817. When we talk prior to my drawing up the contract, I have my buyer determine the maximum amount per month (mortgage, plus taxes and insurance) he's able to pay, and I get back with him later. I usually try to go $50 below the maximum amount, as a built-in cushion for my buyer.

What if your tenant refinances after five years? You know you've made good money in interest over the five years, but what will you have made on that $50,000 loan when you cash out of it? I love this part. You can also calculate this amount on your hp 12c. Using the same figures, on the $475 mortgage payment that will take 21.08 years to pay off:

f, then CLX
50000, then CHS then PV
21, then g, then n (you can't do fractions of years)
10, then g, then i
PMT (this comes up 475.39)
475, then PMT, then n
253 (21.08 years) comes up

Now, what if they refinance in five years? Leave the current numbers in there, and press

5, then g, then n, then FV (future value)
45,482.83 (round up to 45,483) is what you'll get at the closing

So here's the bottom line. You've made money for five years, at $475/month in principal and interest. That total is $28,500. Add that to the $45,483 you receive at closing, and your $50,000 contract sale has earned you a grand total of $73,983 in five years. It's truly a beautiful thing. If they refinance after ten years, your total is $95,050.

So what's the disadvantage to land contract sales? First of all, there's always the chance the buyer will default and you'll get the house back. However, if they've taken care of the home (do your occasional checks!), the worst that can happen is you'll keep their deposit and resell the house. Another disadvantage I see is doing land contracts with complete strangers. Most of my buyers have been solid tenants whom I trust.

I sold one of my duplexes to a family that wanted to convert it into a single family home. I gave them the go-ahead on the conversion. These people seemed like good candidates, although I didn't know them well. They had no credit, but a good work history. They gave me $2000 down, and five months into the contract and half way into the conversion, they called from Missouri. They'd moved out! He'd gotten in a hassle with his boss and quit. Unfortunately, the down payment didn't begin to cover the remaining work. I should've known better (dumbass attack # 1078).

Single-family homes are easier to sell on contract than multi-family homes. Although I think it's a great idea to buy a duplex, live in one half and rent the other half out, thus covering your mortgage payment, most buyers don't want to be landlords. They'd rather buy a single family home. My duplexes are my bread and butter rentals, but I've begun buying more single-family homes with the express purpose of selling them on contract. I wouldn't have been comfortable doing land contracts early in my career, but because I've established solid relationships with many people in my neighborhood, I have tenants (and friends and relatives of tenants) who want to buy homes from me. Since I'm more than mid-way through my career, installment sales represent my intention to change gears and lighten my hands-on work. I don't do any 30-year loans because I don't want anything that long term, but depending on your age and goals, you may structure yours differently.

Beware though, of property tax and insurance increases. If your buyer, on a 30-year loan, is maxed out with what they're paying you monthly and property taxes take a huge jump, which happened here in Indianapolis, what can you do? Stretching that loan out to 40 or even 50 years doesn't lower the payment much. If you know your tenant won't be able to refinance, if you're going to be the bank forever, I'd try to keep the loan to 20 years so there's a little cushion there in the event taxes/insurance costs go up.

To help with tax payments, I file homestead exemptions at the city/county building when I go there to record the installment sale of the property. This exemption lowers the property taxes for the homeowner. Your county auditor or recorder will have the forms. Your buyer won't realize the savings until the following tax year, but it's substantial enough to make it worth going through the filing process.

I'm including a copy of my purchase contract, which I've simplified as much as possible. In a flat real estate market, I see yard signs advertising "no money down" but I'd never go that route. If someone's buying a house from you and doesn't have to put any money down, what makes it any different than renting? They're not invested in the deal, emotionally or financially. I don't accept any less than $1000 down, and I just lowered that from $2000 because the market here is flat right now. When things improve, I'll be raising it back to $2000. The down payment is non-refundable.

I treat my contract buyers like renters in that I check their houses to make sure they're taking good care of them. I'm still the owner, even though they're buying. If I end up getting the house back, I want to make sure it's in good shape. I have one contract buyer right now who is a hoarder. The photos below are of her basement. She told me she needs all that stuff. Pack rat alert! I had to enlist the help of her daughter to convince her it needed to be cleaned up.

What happens if your buyer stops paying? I've not had people default very often, but situations do occur that prevent buyers from being able to honor the contract. They lose jobs, become ill or stop paying for a variety of reasons. Most of the time, they let me know about it ahead of time and begin to move out immediately. I go to the house with a quitclaim deed, which is a simple, one-page form that deeds the house back to me, for zero dollars. Only the buyer's signature is required on this form. I fill it out beforehand, and the buyer and I take it to a Notary Public. After my buyer signs it in the presence of the Notary (there's a small fee for having something notarized), the house is transferred back to me. Of course, it's not legally transferred until I take it to the recorder's office and file it there. Bingo. The property's mine again. After I've touched up paint, etc. at the house, I look for a replacement buyer. The vast majority of defaults occur this way, and the transfer of the property back to the owner goes smoothly. The buyer knows he's unable to continue with the purchase, feels badly about it, and makes arrangements to leave quickly.

Remember my buyer who abandoned the property and called me from Missouri to tell me about it? When that happened, I hadn't filed his contract with the recorder's office yet; there was nothing on file regarding the sale of that home. (Whew!) The buyer had moved everything out and left it spotless, so I resold it a few weeks later to another family. What if I'd recorded the contract? Chasing him down in Missouri with a quitclaim deed in hand wouldn't have been an option. Instead, I would've had my attorney file for a cancellation of the contract, as in the case below.

What if your buyer isn't paying and doesn't leave? This rarely happens. If you're sure he's incapable of getting caught up on the payment, you might try bribing him out by offering a couple hundred dollars if he clears everything out by a certain date. With foreclosure looming in his immediate future, this tactic often works. If he doesn't bite, you'll have to involve your attorney and have him file a cancellation of the contract. This is quicker, easier and cheaper than foreclosure and usually does the trick. The tenant receives an official letter from your attorney regarding the suit; he's given the option to hire an attorney and respond within 21 days. If there's no response, a court order gives the property back to the owner. Most tenants start moving out when they receive the letter from the attorney. They know they're behind in rent and, if there's no fault on your part as the owner, there's no point in their hiring an attorney. Also, if they're already behind in their payments, it's doubtful they have extra money to hire an attorney. If they don't move, they're subject to being moved out by the Sheriff and having their possessions put in storage, at their expense. The cancellation of the contract process usually takes at least a couple months and a few hundred dollars, but is less costly and time-consuming than a foreclosure.

If the tenant has stopped paying and doesn't intend to leave, for whatever reason, you'll need to have your attorney start the foreclosure process. I've never known this to happen, but it's possible. If the tenant files bankruptcy during the process, this will complicate things further. I've never had to foreclose on anyone, and would do my best to avoid it if possible. Foreclosures can drag out over several months, even years in some cases.

So, back to selling your house on contract…After you've met with your buyer and read through all the papers, signed the necessary forms and gone to the Notary, you may take the contract to the offices of the county auditor and recorder so they can be filed. You also have to bring whatever disclosure forms are required by the state when you sell a property; the federal government requires a lead base paint disclosure, and my state requires a sales disclosure form. Your county auditor will know what forms you'll need to bring.

My buyer, when we're finished, has the following items in his possession:

- A copy of the land contract (not necessary to have notarized)
- A list of my trusted repair people
- Lead-base paint pamphlet issued by the government
- Two sets of keys to the house
- Pride and happiness in being given the opportunity to buy a home

I've had people in tears after being given the keys to their homes. These are people who never dreamed they'd be able to own a home. Although land contracts are a great moneymaker for me, providing these dream homes for my buyers makes me feel part of something wonderful…for these families, the neighborhood and the city as well. I love it.

The major advantages to land contracts are the following:

- I don't have to claim all the profit in the year I sell the property; it's spread out over the life of the loan (check this out with your tax advisor)
- I have no responsibility for repairs or bill-paying at the property
- The buyers are invested in it financially and emotionally, therefore motivated to take good care of it
- Being the bank enables me to make more money on the sale, through principal and interest, than I would by selling outright
- Land contracts provide long-term income, with little work involved
- As your buyer makes payments to you over time, he's establishing a good credit history for himself, which may enable him to qualify for a traditional mortgage at a lower interest rate

Once you've gotten your paperwork done and filed everything at the courthouse, you should be able to put things on cruise control. You'll need to touch base with your buyer, make sure things are running smoothly at the house, and check to see they're maintaining it well, inside and out. But beyond that, just sit back and enjoy the ride.

When your buyer has made his last payment, give him a Warranty Deed to the house, a sample of which I'm including here. This officially transfers ownership to him, and will need to be notarized. He may choose to record it on his own. I also write out a receipt stating the contract has been paid in full.

I'm including a copy of a land contract and a quitclaim deed, to give you an idea of what's involved. I've simplified the language where possible. *Check with your real estate attorney regarding what type of contract is appropriate in your jurisdiction.*

PURCHASE CONTRACT

Parcel No._____Lot Size_____

This agreement has been made on the_____day of_____
by (Seller) and _____ (Buyer).
Seller hereby sells to Buyer the following described real estate, together
with all improvements thereon, located in Marion County, Indiana,
more particularly described as follows:

Subject also to all roadways, easements, rights of way, legal drains,
restrictions, covenants and agreements of record and current taxes not
delinquent.

1) PURCHASE PRICE AND MANNER OF PAYMENT
a. The purchase price for the real estate will be_____dollars
    ($_____) which Buyer (jointly, if more than one) agrees
    to pay Seller in accordance with the terms and conditions of this
    agreement.
b. The purchase price will be paid in the following manner: a down
    payment of _____dollars ($_____) will
    be paid to Seller by Buyer, and Seller acknowledges receipt of such
    payment. The remaining unpaid balance of the purchase price will
    be paid to Seller with an interest rate of _____ (_____%)
    per annum, in monthly payments of _____dollars
    ($_____). The first payment will be made on or before the
    first day of _____, _____, with like
    payments being due on or before the first day of each month until
    the remainder of the purchase price, both principal and interest,
    has been paid in full. Buyer may make prepayments, after three
    years from the date of this agreement.
c. All payments must be made to Seller at: Barnes Properties, address
    here. Payments may be made with a money order or a check. Cash
    will not be accepted. Keep your money order receipt as proof of
    payment.
d. Buyer must pay, in addition to the above payments, a late fee in
    the amount of _____ ($_____) for any payment not

received at the above address by the 5th day of the month. On the 10th day, we can file in Court to cancel this agreement and obtain possession of the property, and if we do, the Buyer is responsible for all court costs, attorney fees, and any other expenses involved as a result of Purchaser's breach of this Contract.

2) TAXES AND INSURANCE, UTILITIES, REPAIRS

a. Buyer will be responsible for taxes and insurance on the real estate, beginning with the first payment. Seller will continue to pay taxes and insurance on behalf of Buyer, and agrees to provide insurance on the real estate until such time as Buyer obtains insurance on the property. In addition to the monthly principal and interest payment of $_____, Buyer will pay Seller, each month, an amount equal to 1/12th of the annual taxes and insurance payable on the property. This amount is currently $_____, making the total payment due each month to Seller $_____. This amount can rise or fall if taxes and/or insurance rates change. Buyer promises to make these payments on time each month.

b. Buyer will pay all utility bills associated with the property, and pay them in a timely manner.

c. All maintenance and repairs will be the responsibility of the Buyer. Buyer will keep the premises—interior and exterior—clean and well maintained.

3) EVIDENCE OF TITLE

As evidence of title, Seller agrees to furnish either an abstract of title or a policy of owner's title insurance upon signing of this agreement, at Buyer's request. Any further evidence of Title hereafter will be obtained at the expense of the Buyer.

4) WARRANTIES OF SELLER

Seller warrants that Seller has good title to the real estate, free and clear of any liens, leases, restrictions and encumbrances, except as follows:

Easements and restrictions of record as disclosed in the Title Binder

Current real estate taxes not yet delinquent.

Seller has made no contract to sell all or part of the real estate to any other person other than the Buyer. There are no unpaid bills for labor done on the property. There are no existing violations of zoning ordinances or other restrictions applicable to the real estate. There is no judgment of any court of the state or country that is or may become a lien on the property.

5) TRANSFER OF BUYER'S INTEREST--CONDEMNATION, assigned, pledged, mortgaged, encumbered or transferred by Buyer without written consent of Seller. If the real estate or any part thereof is taken or damaged pursuant to an exercise or threat of exercise of the power of eminent domain, the entire proceeds of the compensation are hereby assigned to the Seller. Proceeds will be applied in part or entirely as a prepayment of the contract balance or to restoration of the real estate. If electing this option pays the balance in full, then Seller will pay the remaining balance of the compensation to the Buyer.

6) MECHANIC'S LIENS
Buyer will not permit any Statement of Intention to hold a Mechanic's Lien to be filed against the real estate nor against any interest therein by reason of labor, services or materials claimed to have been performed or furnished to or for the Buyer.

7) INDEMNIFICATION AND RELEASE
Regardless of whether or not separate, several, joint or concurrent liability may be imposed on Seller, Buyer will indemnify and release Seller from and against all damages, claims and liability rising from or connected with Buyer's control or use of the property, including any damage to person or property. This indemnification will not include any matter for which the Seller is protected against by insurance. If Seller, without fault, becomes a party to litigation commenced by or against the Buyer, Buyer will hold Seller harmless. Buyer hereby releases Seller from all liability for any accident, damage or injury caused to person or property on or about the real estate, excepting liability of Seller for her negligence and notwithstanding whether such acts or omission be active or passive.

8) USE OF REAL ESTATE BY TENANT

The real estate will not be rented, leased or occupied by persons other than _____

None of the improvements located on the property will be changed without the permission of the Seller. Buyer will use the real estate carefully and keep it in good repair. With respect to occupancy and use of the property, Buyer will obey all laws, ordinances and regulations of any government authority having jurisdiction in the area.

a. Until the purchase price and all interest is paid in full, Seller has the right to enter and inspect the property at reasonable times, on advance notice.

b. Buyer assumes all risk and responsibility for accident, injury or damage to person or property arising from Buyer's use and control of the real estate. Buyer will insure against such risk by carrying standard liability insurance (this is automatically part of renters' insurance policy) in such amounts as are satisfactory to Seller, insuring Seller's liability as well as the Buyer.

9) DEFAULT AND ACCELERATION

Upon the occurrence of any Event of Default (below) the entire contract balance will become immediately payable, without any protest by the Buyer. Seller may pursue all options available by law, to collect such balance and interest, to foreclose this Purchase Agreement. The following items are Events of Default:

a. Default by Buyer for a period of ten (10) days in the monthly payment.

b. Default for a period of ten (10) days after written notice thereof is given to Buyer in the performance or observation of any term of this agreement.

c. Lease or encumbrance of the real estate other than as expressly permitted by this agreement, or the making of any levy, seizure or attachment thereof, or a substantial, uninsured loss of any part of the real estate.

d. Buyer begins insolvency or bankruptcy proceedings, makes an assignment for the benefit of creditors, or admits in writing the inability to pay debts as they become due.

e. Any part of real estate or Buyer assets is placed in the hands of any receiver, Trustee or other officers of any court, or Buyer agrees to the appointment of any such receiver.

f. Desertion of real estate.

g. Actual or threatened alteration, demolition or removal of any improvements.

h. Sale or transfer of Buyer's interest in the real estate or any part thereof without Seller's written consent.

i. Failure to follow any of the terms of this agreement. It is agreed by Buyer that, unless Buyer has paid the Purchase Agreement in full, Seller may cancel this agreement and take possession of the real estate if the Buyer defaults. Seller will keep all monies paid by Buyer toward purchase price as an agreed payment for Buyer's possession of the real estate prior to the default. Seller may recover damages for unlawful detention of the real estate after default, for any failure to pay taxes or insurance, for failure to maintain the real estate, for waste committed thereon, or for any other damages suffered by Seller, including attorneys' fees and court costs incurred in the default period.

10) ADDITIONAL COVENANTS AND REPRESENTATIONS OF SELLER

Upon payment by Buyer of the purchase price in full, with all interest and conditions of this agreement, Seller will convey the real estate to Buyer by Warranty Deed, subject only to easements and restrictions on record as of the date of this agreement; to the rights of persons in possession; to the lien of all taxes and assessments payable by Buyer; and to any other encumbrances which, by the terms of this agreement, are to be paid by the Buyer.

11) GENERAL AGREEMENT OF THE PARTIES

This contract will extend to and be binding upon the heirs, personal representatives, successors and assigns of the parties. When applicable, use of the singular form of any word also will apply to the plural. Any notices to be given hereunder will be deemed sufficiently given when actually served on the person to be notified, or placed in an envelope directed to the person to be notified at the following address and deposited in the U.S. Mail by certified or registered mail, prepaid.

If to Seller, at payments address.

If to Buyer, at: _____

Change of address will be given in writing prior to the change.

IN WITNESS THEREOF, Seller and Buyer have executed this instrument on this_____day of_____,_____.

_____   _____
Buyer   Seller

_____   _____
Buyer (printed)   Seller (printed)

STATE OF INDIANA   )
                                                   );
COUNTY OF   )

Before me, a Notary Public in and for said County and State, personally appeared _____
and_____, who acknowledged the execution of the foregoing, and who, having been duly sworn, stated that any representations therein contained are true.

Witness my hand and Notarial Seal this__day of_____,____.

_____, Notary Public

Resident of_____County

My Commission expires:

_____

PARCEL NO._____

QUITCLAIM DEED

THIS INDENTURE WITNESSETH, That _____
_____ (Grantor)
of_____County, in the State of _____
QUITCLAIM(S) to _____
_____ (Grantee)
of_____County, in the State of_____,
for the sum of_____Dollars ($_____)
and other valuable consideration, the receipt and sufficiency of which is
hereby acknowledged, the following described real estate in_____
County, State of _____:

The address of such real estate is commonly known as _____
_____
Tax bills should be sent to Grantee at such address unless otherwise
indicated below.
IN WITNESS WHEREOF, Grantor has executed this deed this
_____day of_____,_____.

Grantor: (SEAL) Grantor: (SEAL)
Signature _____ Signature _____
Printed _____ Printed _____

STATE OF

                        SS: ACKNOWLEDGMENT

COUNTY OF

Before me a Notary Public in and for said County and State, personally
appeared_____
who acknowledged the execution of the foregoing Quitclaim Deed, and
who, having been duly sworn, stated that any representations therein
contained are true.

Witness my hand and Notarial Seal this_____day of_____
_____,_____.

My commission expires: Signature_____

_____   Printed _____ ,

Notary Public, Resident of_____County,_____ .

This instrument prepared by_____ ,

Return deed to _____

Send tax bills to _____

WARRANTY DEED

THIS INDENTURE WITNESSETH, that _____
(Grantor(s) of _____County, _____
conveys and warrants to _____
(Grantee(s) of_____County,_____
for the sum of One Dollar ($1.00) and other valuable consideration,
the receipt of which is hereby acknowledged, the following-described
real estate in _____
County, _____ .

(legal description of property)

Subject to all Mortgages, Liens, Taxes, Assessments and Encumbrances
of Record.

More commonly known as (street address):

IN WITNESS WHEREOF, the Grantor(s) has (have) executed this
deed, this_____day of_____,_____.

_____   _____

GRANTOR   GRANTOR

STATE OF _____)
) SS:
COUNTY OF _____)

Before me, a Notary Public in and for said County and State, personally
appeared_____
Grantor(s) who acknowledged the execution of the foregoing, and
who, having been duly sworn, stated that any representations therein
contained are true.

Witness my hand and Notarial Seal this_____day of_____
_____,_____.
_____Notary Public
Resident of _____County, _____

My Commission expires:

Return Deed to: _____

Send Tax Bills to: _____

This Instrument Prepared by: _____

What if the property you're selling on contract is one you've owned less than a year? You'll have to pay capital gains at 28, or 33, or whatever percent tax bracket you are, unless you can put off the actual sale until the one-year mark has passed. This can be accomplished by using a lease-option agreement with your buyer.

The lease-option is another popular selling strategy I'd like to cover with you. It differs from the land contract in that it's not an *immediate* sale. Your tenant agrees to buy the home he's living in at an agreed-on price, at a set date in the future. In the case above, you can start your buyer out with a lease-option and switch him over to the land contract when the one-year date has passed. He'll give you the down payment and take over all responsibilities at the house, as detailed in the option agreement I'm including here. After you've owned the property for one year, you can sign the land contract papers with him at the agreed-upon price, and proceed as above.

Most investors use the lease option as follows. It works well for someone who can't quite qualify for a traditional loan right now but feels they'll be able to in one to three years, or whatever time frame is set up between you and the buyer. He signs a lease agreement, which is like your normal rental agreement. Many investors keep the option as a separate agreement from the rental agreement.

The option includes a small non-refundable down payment, at least $500-1000. What makes the lease-option attractive to the buyer is this:

- The sale price of the house is locked in when the option is signed, even if the sale isn't going to occur for three or more years.
- A portion of each month's rent is put toward the down payment for the house. For those who find it difficult to save up for a down payment, this is an easy way to work toward being a homeowner
- They don't *have* to exercise the option to purchase the house. At any time during the option period, if they change their minds they can walk away.

For the seller, the lease-option can be a good thing if you're fairly sure your buyer will be able to get a mortgage within the option time frame. You might ask them to get a mortgage preapproval. This is inexpensive, and will determine how much they can afford to pay on a mortgage per month. It will give you an idea if they'll qualify to be future buyers of your property.

As the seller, make sure you charge higher rent than normal when you're doing a lease-option. After all, part of it's going toward the down payment. For the buyer, it has to be worth it in terms of how much per month is going to the down payment, so if your rent is usually $800/month, I'd jack it up to $1000/month but tell them $200 of it's going to the down payment. If you charge them an upfront down payment of $1000 with the option, after three years they'd have $8200 toward the down payment. That's pretty impressive. Throughout the option time period, you retain ownership of the property and treat everything as you would if the tenants were just renting from you. If the tenant violates any part of the lease agreement, you may file eviction in the small claims court, just as you would with any renter.

There are some disadvantages to the lease-option, however, if you're the seller:

- If you sign an option agreement, you can't back out. Your tenant can change his mind, but you're locked in no matter what.
- An option is usually for a certain price. What if values skyrocket? You'll be selling below market value by the time the option gets exercised. What if the market goes way down? Your tenants may back out, saying the house is over-priced. You can build in an inflation clause and make it reciprocal, to protect both parties. But remember, the tenant can back out. You can't.
- There are the usual disadvantages that also apply to renters, namely inability to pay due to loss of job, illness or other personal problems, but in that case, you'd keep their option money and try again with another buyer.
- As time goes on and the buyer feels he's not going to be able to meet the requirements to buy the house, he may become resentful of the high rent he's been paying, and decide he's going to get even by damaging the property before abandoning it.
- The actual sale of the property is delayed by the length of the option period.

There are two reasons I prefer land contracts to lease-options. First of all, I'd much prefer completing the sale than drawing it out over a period of a year or more. (A bird in the hand...) I like the done deal concept, rather than waiting and wondering whether my tenant will actually stay through the option period or be able to take the house off my hands when the option period is done. Secondly, many of my buyers won't qualify for a traditional mortgage in the near future. A lease-option wouldn't help them buy a house. Look at your tenant mix; hopefully, some of your current renters may become future buyers. Their financial situations will dictate whether the land contract or lease-option is a better choice for you, if you choose to be the bank.

I'm including a sample of a lease option; again, check with your real estate attorney regarding what forms are used in your area.

OPTION TO PURCHASE AGREEMENT

This Option to Purchase Agreement is made on _____
between _____ (Seller/Landlord) and
_____ (Buyer/Tenant).

Whereas, Seller/Landlord is the fee owner of certain real property being,
lying and situated in_____County,_____,
such real property having a street address of _____
(the "Property").

Whereas Seller/Landlord and Buyer/Tenant have together executed
a prior Lease Agreement, the subject of which is the aforementioned
Property (the "Lease Agreement").

Now, therefore, for and in consideration of the convenience and
obligation contained herein, the Seller/Landlord hereby grants to Buyer/
Tenant an exclusive option to purchase the aforementioned "Property".
The parties agree as follows:

1) OPTION TERM. The Option to Purchase Agreement commences
on _____and expires at 11:59PM on_____ .

2) NOTICE REQUIRED TO EXERIZE OPTION. To exercise
the Option to Purchase, the Buyer/Tenant must deliver to the Seller/
Landlord written notice of Buyer/Tenant's intent to purchase. In
addition, the notice must specify a valid closing date. The closing must
occur before the original expiration date of the Lease Agreement, or the
expiration date of the Option to Purchase Agreement in Paragraph 1,
whichever occurs later.

3) OPTION CONSIDERATION. The Buyer/Tenant shall pay the
Seller/Landlord a non-refundable fee of $_____, receipt of
which is hereby acknowledged by Seller/Landlord. This amount shall
be credited to the purchase price at closing if the Buyer/Tenant timely
exercises the Option to Purchase, provided that the Buyer/Tenant (a) is
not in default of the Lease Agreement, and (b) closes the conveyance of

the Property. The Seller/Landlord shall not refund the fee if the Buyer/ Tenant defaults, fails to close, or does not execute the Option.

4) PURCHASE PRICE. The total purchase price for the property is $_____. Provided the Lease and Option are abided by, the Seller/Landlord shall credit toward the purchase price at closing the sum of $_____ from each monthly lease payment the Buyer/Tenant timely made. The Buyer/Tenant shall receive no credit at closing for any monthly lease payment received after the due date specified in the Lease Agreement.

5) EXCLUSIVITY OF OPTION. This Option to Purchase Agreement is exclusive and non-assignable. Should Buyer/Tenant attempt to assign, convey, delegate or transfer this Option without the Seller/Landlord's written consent, any such attempt shall be deemed null and void.

6) CLOSING AND SETTLEMENT. Seller/Landlord shall determine the title company at which closing shall occur and shall inform Buyer/ Tenant of the location in writing. All closing costs shall be the sole responsibility of the Buyer/Tenant, except for the pro-rated share of the ad valorem taxes due at the time of closing, for which the Seller/ Landlord is solely responsible.

7) FINANCING AND AVAILABILITY. Seller/Landlord makes no representation or warranties as to the availability of financing regarding this Option to Purchase. Buyer/Tenant is solely responsible for obtaining financing in order to exercise this Option.

8) FINANCING DISCLAIMER. The parties acknowledge that it is impossible to predict the availability of financing toward the purchase of this property. Obtaining financing shall not be held as a condition of this Option to Purchase Agreement.

9) REMEDIES UPON DEFAULT. If Buyer/Tenant defaults under this Option to Purchase Agreement or Lease Agreement, then in addition to any other remedies available to Seller/Landlord at law or in equity, Seller/Landlord may terminate this Option to Purchase Agreement by giving written notice of the termination. The Buyer/Tenant shall

lose entitlement to any refund of rent or option consideration. For this Option to Purchase Agreement to be enforceable and effective, Buyer/Tenant must comply with all terms of the Lease Agreement.

10) COMMISSION. No real estate commission or other commission shall be paid in connection with this transaction.

11) RECORDING OF AGREEMENT. Buyer/Tenant shall not record this Option to Purchase Agreement on the Public Records of any public office without the express and written consent of Seller/Landlord.

12) ACKNOWLEDGEMENT. The parties are executing this Option to Purchase Agreement voluntarily and without any duress or undue influence. The parties have carefully read this Agreement and have asked any question needed to understand its terms, consequences and binding effects, and fully understand them, and have been given a copy. The parties have sought the advice of an attorney if so desired prior to signing this Agreement.

13) TIMING. Timing is of the essence in this Option to Purchase Agreement.

14) GOVERNING LAW AND VENUE. This Option to Purchase Agreement shall be governed, construed and interpreted by, through and under the Laws of the State of _____. The parties agree that the venue for any and all disputes related to this Option to Purchase Agreement shall be _____ County, _____ .

15) OPTION TO PURCHASE CONTROLLING. In the event a conflict arises between the terms and condition of the Lease Agreement and the Option to Purchase Agreement, the Option to Purchase Agreement shall control.

16) ENTIRE AGREEMENT; MODIFICATION. This Agreement sets forth the entire Agreement and understanding between the parties and supersedes all prior discussions. No modification to this Option to Purchase Agreement nor any waiver of any rights under this Option to

Purchase Agreement will be effective unless in writing, signed by the party to be charged.

SELLER/LANDLORD
SIGN _____
PRINT _____

BUYER/TENANT
SIGN _____
PRINT _____

BUYER/TENANT
SIGN _____
PRINT _____

THE BOTTOM LINE

At the end of each year, I like to look at where my business has taken me and make a pros and cons list. I usually have a property or two I'm dissatisfied with for one reason or another...maybe I need to sell one, or make some major improvements at another. I formulate a plan for the coming year partially based on what's worked and what hasn't. The only sure thing in this business is change. And speaking of change, I'd suggest you speak with your accountant about selling/exit strategies before proceeding. Tax laws are constantly changing, and tax changes may greatly impact your bottom line when you sell your property.

Although flipping properties used to be a hot strategy, many investors got burned when the market began to plummet. I like to use flipping sparingly, in conjunction with buying and holding. It's not a guaranteed income source, and the tax ramifications can be significant. Selling outright is a smart way to free up money to pay down debt or buy additional property.

Installment sales are a nice way to create a steady income stream without the daily duties associated with rentals. The risk of default is balanced by knowing your buyer and getting a hefty down payment.

As you move through your real estate investing career, success will follow you if you're open to fresh ideas, plan well, and change gears when needed. The economy has its ups and downs, the real estate market fluctuates, and your chosen neighborhood will see various changes through the years. Being flexible and thinking outside the box will serve you well. If you change gears and aren't comfortable, you can always take a different path altogether. Keep growing professionally, explore the opportunities and see where they take you!

CHAPTER THIRTEEN
YOU CAN DO THIS

REAL ESTATE INVESTING WAS never part of the plan. The twists and turns of life present unexpected challenges, and little did I know my career would begin with the purchase of a small, one-story fixer-upper I bought after the death of my son many years ago. In those early days, I read several books and networked with other investors and professionals, to increase my learning curve. If you've read this book and others, you're on your way as well. Don't be shy about asking local professionals for help; they possess a wealth of information that can't be found in reading material.

At this writing, I'm still working on that learning curve... A couple times each year, assess where you are, personally and professionally. Changes in these areas will lead you down new paths in your real estate investing journey. With each passing year, changes in my investment goals present new challenges and learning opportunities. As I mentioned earlier, the economy is always in a state of flux, and so is the world of real estate investing.

My tenants through the years have enabled me to grow in numerous ways. I've sharpened my negotiating and interpersonal skills, increased my ability to laugh at myself and the craziness of this world, and developed a deeper appreciation for the human tie that binds my tenants and me. Although some of their antics drive me crazy, the vast majority of my tenants are lovely, hardworking people, and the relationships I've developed with them through the years have truly enriched my life. Providing clean, well-maintained homes for these people makes me feel

I'm contributing something worthwhile to their lives, the community and the city as well.

I love my work. It affords me autonomy, freedom and flexibility… precious commodities. And of course, the money's not bad either… whether you choose to do it part- or full-time, investing in affordable rental properties will provide steady income and build wealth for your future. So, although real estate investing was never part of the plan, I live and breathe it every day, and hope this book has instilled in you a sense of excitement about the opportunities that exist for you, too.

I wish you the very best as you embark on your journey into real estate investing. If you have questions or comments about the material in this book, you may contact me at <u>barbarabarnesgetty@indy.rr.com</u>. I'll do my best to respond in a timely manner. You are the hero of your own story, as I am of mine. Prepare well, trust yourself and go for it!

Made in the USA
San Bernardino, CA
05 February 2014